A MOTHER'S STORY OF CARNAGE,
COURAGE, AND THE TRIUMPH OF FAITH

WHEN THE BOUGH BREAKS

NANCY FERRARO

Dear Donna,

WHEN

THE

BOUGH

BREAKS

Wishing you light ~

a memoir

love,   *Nancy*

NANCY FERRARO

woodhall press

Woodhall Press
Norwalk, CT

woodhall press

Woodhall Press, 81 Old Saugatuck Road, Norwalk, CT 06855
WoodhallPress.com
Copyright © 2022 Nancy Ferraro

Cover design: Asha Hossain
Layout artist: Amie McCracken
Leaf image: azerbaijan_stockers

Library of Congress Cataloging-in-Publication Data available

ISBN 978-1-954907-44-7 (paper: alk paper)
ISBN 978-1-954907-45-4 (electronic)

First Edition
Distributed by Independent Publishers Group
(800) 888-4741

Printed in the United States of America

This is a work of creative nonfiction. All of the events in this memoir are true to the best of the author's memory. Some names and identifying features have been changed to protect the identity of certain parties. Names, characters, places, and incidents either are the product of the author's imagination or are used fictitiously. Any resemblances to actual persons, living or dead, events, or locales is entirely coincidental. The author in no way represents any company, corporation, or brand, mentioned herein. The views expressed in this memoir are solely those of the author.

TABLE OF CONTENTS

Foreword xi
Preface xv
Prologue xix
1 The Oldest Profession 1
2 The Families 5
3 The Nod 9
4 Logic Is Relative 23
5 Approved for What? 31
6 Caroline . . . Not Caroline 33
7 Gestation 37
8 Welcome to Transylvania 43
9 Lollipops at Thirty Thousand Feet 49
10 Loving George 53
11 This Is Not How to Do Second Grade 65
12 George's First American Christmas 69
13 Doctor Shopping in the Land of Denial 73
14 Maybe My Mother Was Right .77
15 Chemistry Lessons 81
16 The Winter of My Discontent .83
17 Enter "The Emperor" 87
18 Chemistry Meets Vodka 89
19 The Report's in the Drawer 95
20 Sometimes, Extinction Is a Good Thing 99
21 Between a Rock and a Hard Place 101
22 Help! Help? 105
23 So Close... 113
24 Escape Artistry in Three Easy Steps 119
25 Mommy Dearest 125
26 Cooking . . . Not for the Meek 131
27 I Want Me, Too 135
28 What Do You Call a Whale Watch with No Whales? 139
29 My Heart Skipped a Beat 145
30 Welcome to the Hotel California 147
31 My Whirling Dervish and His Mantra 155
32 It Takes a Village . . . Or the Entire Hospital Staff 163
33 Even the Mayor Can Wear Out His Welcome 167
34 Summertime and the Living 175
35 Help? Thanks. Wow! 181
36 Gummy Bears and Pink Frosted Doughnuts 183
37 The End . . . Or the Beginning 185
Epilogue 189
Acknowledgments 193
About the Author 195

AUTHOR'S NOTE

There are three sides to every story: your side, my side, and the truth. And no one is lying. Memories shared serve each differently.

It seems appropriate that this quote would be attributed to Robert Evans, the movie producer known for telling iconic stories through film, like *Rosemary's Baby* and *The Godfather*. These stories—all stories, in fact—are a reflection of somebody's truth. And they are all valuable, because we are a people who need to connect through shared experience.

Which leads me to this: This book was written to shed light, share hope, and reach out to those who are now where I was—in a hopeless, dark, and lonely tunnel. It was written to start a conversation about an infinite number of topics, including trauma, adoption, alcoholism, family dysfunction, developmental disabilities, empathy, love, perseverance in the face of certain defeat, and ultimately, hope. A memoir reflects the author's recollections. Some names have been changed, some dialogue recreated. But this is my truth, as I remember it. I invite you to enjoy it in the spirit of shedding light, offering hope and connection. You are not alone.

You own everything that happened to you. Tell your stories.
If people wanted you to write warmly about them,
they should have behaved better.
Anne Lamott, *Bird by Bird: Some Instructions on Writing and Life*

FOREWORD

Nancy Ferraro's *When the Bough Breaks* is a profoundly moving and emotional account of a mother's journey down the complex pathway of raising an extremely developmentally challenged youth from one of the world's most notorious child orphanage systems, under the brutal regime of Nicolae Ceaușescu in Romania. All children with developmental disabilities were placed in these "child concentration and death camps," where terrible atrocities took place. Americans rushed to the aid of these children following the Romanian Revolution in 1989–1990, when the "hidden secrets" of Romanian state-run institutions, known as *camin spitals*, were uncovered and posted on every news channel around the world.

These very special children were the by-product of "population control" under the Ceaușescu fascist regime. The majority of these children had normal developmental delays, but with ongoing institutionalization, abuse, and neglect, as well as starvation and the government's annihilation program of the children (by attrition), they developed even more profound patterns of what is known as "traumatic autism." Combined with profound childhood developmental trauma disorder, this led to a pattern of "global developmental delays." As stated, multiple Americans flocked to Romania to attempt to "rescue the children" from the huge problems they faced, many ultimately disrupting the adoptions and placing the children in American state care when they discovered the issues were far greater than any family could handle.

Nancy Ferraro emotionally describes her experience of adopting her son George from Romania. He was clearly feral in nature and would have been deemed "irrecuperable" in any other institutional setting around the world. Nancy recounts her entire journey from start to finish, including issues most parents could not even conceive of—violence, aggression, regressive behaviors, lack of fundamental cognitive and psychosocial skills, as well as no functional "emotional intelligence or attachment" were battles that she faced head-on. Nancy also faced many naysayers and unknowing or untrained therapists, doctors, educators, and even friends and family who felt that "love would conquer all" without understanding the unbelievable task of living with a child who has been so profoundly neurologically and psychologically damaged that even day-to-day activities were a challenge.

Nancy persevered and brought her story to the attention of many. She faced an abundance of criticism, denial, and people telling her to "just give up," but because of her tenacity and strong faith in the human spirit, along with her dedication to her son George, a compromise was reached for Nancy and her family, whereby George would be brought to the highest possible functional level to become a productive member of society, despite his coexisting disabilities.

When the Bough Breaks is not only Nancy's story; it's the story of literally thousands of parents who have adopted children from extremely deprived Eastern European institutional settings, particularly Romania, which will go down in history as the site of the "second Holocaust of children" perpetrated by a fascist regime.

I have spent years working with the international charity known as Care for Children International, working as a triage officer in well over 240 of these profoundly damaging institutions with the hope of finding children who would be able to be rehabilitated and eventually mainstreamed to achieve a higher level of functioning.

On a more personal note, I myself have adopted eight children from these terrible institutional settings. They started off very much like George and are now functional human beings, although not without the remnants of profound childhood developmental trauma that will persist throughout their entire lives.

I believe the goal of this book is to bring to light the importance of objective parenting, diligence, and acceptance of certain inevitabilities, while also being true to one's own journey, which will often be shot down by others or grossly misunderstood. *When the Bough Breaks* is a story of trauma, chaos, hope, recovery, and remediation, accomplished within a family context with very few well-trained medical and psychological professionals, which continues today.

I hope that this book will be shared with any and all parents who have experienced similar adoption situations, many of whom may have hidden their experiences and not told their stories. I also hope it will be shared with professionals working in the field, expanding their knowledge so they can better serve these children and their families.

Nancy Ferraro is to be admired for delivering an extremely accurate, emotional, and personal story, one that stands out among the thousands I've heard in my thirty-five years as an international expert and hands-on international charity worker around the globe.

—Dr. Ronald S. Federici, Board-Certified Neuropsychologist
Professor Emeritus of Child Development and Neuropsychology
President and CEO, Care for Children International, Inc.
Father of eight older adopted children from traumatic backgrounds
Foster parent to forty children
Professional doctor to more than eight thousand damaged souls

PREFACE

When I adopted a four-year-old boy from Romania, I was full of dreams for the life I would give a disadvantaged child and how he would complete my little family. I thought I was giving my son a little brother. All the medical reports said that he was normal, except for a slight speech delay.

George arrived in the suburbs of New Jersey a feral child, a wild animal in the body of a boy. The violence he rained down on us, his new family, nearly destroyed us and everything I assumed motherhood to be. With a host of conditions ranging from fetal alcohol syndrome to institutionally acquired autism, we came to call our new family member "Hurricane George."

When things go awry with our children, society tends to judge the mothers. But we mothers judge ourselves most harshly. Ultimately, I learned that asking for help is not a sign of weakness, but rather, one of courage and strength. In telling this story, I hope to share that sense of comfort with you, my reader.

In this book I take a raw, honest look at the painful—and sometimes humorous—moments of tragedy, trying to bring light to that dark place where it seems there is no end to our children's troubles. This book is for caregivers who find themselves at that bough-breaking moment, the moment when we must redefine our relationships with our children.

I'm not an angel. I'm not a victim. And I'm certainly not a hero.

I'm just a mom who, whether by happenstance or mistake, was plunged into a nightmare and lived to tell the tale, one of heartbreak, hopelessness, and eventual redemption.

Welcome to my journey.

Rock-a-bye, baby,
On the treetop,
When the wind blows,
The cradle will rock.
When the bough breaks,
The cradle will fall, and
Down will come baby,
Cradle and all.

—Traditional American lullaby

PROLOGUE

"C'mon, Bella. Let's go for a walk."

A surprised dog leaps at the phrase she hasn't heard in almost a decade.

I had been expecting a crisp, apple-pie-and-football, leaves-crunching-under-your-boots kind of day. But the morning dawns so clear and uncharacteristically warm that the weather seems to be whispering in my ear, "Be happy. Be at peace."

I cannot.

I awaken that Thanksgiving morning, the month after George's thirteenth birthday, the first Thanksgiving in nine years, to stillness. Coffee in the pot, a puttering husband, newspaper waiting to be perused. Missing is the screaming: *What time Mom-Mom's house? Go now. I want me. Go now.* In the language that has become one of my disabled child's only means of communication, George is demanding to leave for his grandmother's house, my mother-in-law Muriel, immediately, not at the appointed time.

But right now, it is so quiet, I think I must be in the wrong house.

I have spent these last nine years in a state of perpetual crisis, putting out one fire after another, in an attempt to normalize life for the four-year-old boy we adopted from Romania.

The prognoses came in a list: Speech delay. Bipolar disorder. Attention deficit disorder. Attachment disorder. Autism spectrum. Moderate retardation, a term which has now morphed into the very polite and politically correct *developmental disabilities*, yet no less devastating. And, for the final insult, fetal alcohol syndrome.

If the things that were wrong with George were the lyrics of a song, fetal alcohol syndrome would be the chorus. No matter the verses, you're always waiting for the overriding theme, and it just keeps repeating.

If the things that were wrong with George were an ice cream sundae, the FAS would be the cherry. As if all that other shit weren't enough, a disorder that causes children to be violent is certainly the finishing touch.

If the things that were wrong with George were a dream . . . well, *nightmare* doesn't even begin to cover it.

The initial medical reports told us he was normal.

Three weeks ago today, George, now thirteen years old, a child the size of a man, had taken up residence in a group home, a place where he would be cared for with the twenty-four-hour staffing we could not provide for him. Today is the first time we, his family, would be allowed to see or speak to George.

The coffee, the newspaper, the freedom to take the dog for a walk—the normalcy is all too much to process.

Once on the canal towpath, I allow Bella to run, cavort, and explore every scent and insect she can find. I cannot bring myself to rein in the leash, lest she not be able to enjoy this longed-for activity after so many days without.

As the sunshine bathes my face and the almost summery breeze caresses my body, I am overwhelmed. Falling to my knees, sobbing and laughing at the same time, pleasure and guilt intertwined. How could I enjoy this glorious morning, this peaceful hour, when there was still so much left to do for George?

I could not release the yoke of his physical safety from my shoulders. I had not solved George's problems; I had only found people who could help to manage them. The work of recognizing the real tasks at hand and reaping rewards for George is just beginning.

But at this moment, I am recalling the years of judgment by well-meaning family members. Just because George got a joke—like how funny it was to talk into a banana like it was a telephone—didn't mean he would ever learn to read. Or write. Or behave.

Are you sure he's handicapped?

I stopped answering after the fifth query, but the reply was on repeat in my head. *Yes, I'm pretty sure George has special needs.*

When George attacked me, it was somehow my fault.

There's nothing wrong with George. You just don't know how to talk to him.

We would be spending this Thanksgiving Day with some of these same people, my in-laws, who insisted that George's behavior was my doing. Despite this unkindness, my husband Joe held on to this tradition for dear life.

This holiday would not be like any other since George had become a member of our family. This Thanksgiving, George would be delivered to my in-laws' home and then scooped up by the caregivers from his group home. We would see him for four hours, no more, as prescribed by his social worker.

This would be our first time seeing George since his placement. I was excited to see him, but I knew what was coming—the cacophony to which I had become so accustomed. Then, a quiet and uneventful evening, and a blissfully uninterrupted night of sleep.

For George, today would be full of freedom and soda and lots of touching things he had no business touching. Because my war for normalcy was over, I'd released the burden of teaching appropriate behaviors to those who were trained to help this very child. I had won a battle, not knowing what I was fighting for—until now.

I had believed I was fighting for George to have some semblance of order, routine, and discipline, for him to have a happy and well-ordered home life. I'd thought I was fighting for the last remnant of childhood that was left for my son Joey. And I was fighting for my life.

I had long ago stopped fighting for my marriage; that skirmish had been lost before George came along. Although we were still married at the time, Joe and I had lost our marriage years ago.

Our opposing parenting philosophies didn't help. With my little Joey, I was raising the perfect little gentleman, all day long. A boy who said "please" and "thank you" and pushed in his chair when he left the table.

When Joe came home from work and said, "No son of mine will vacuum," he erased my entire day's efforts in ten seconds. While Joe professed to support my parenting philosophy, he failed to deliver. Over the course of a twenty-four year marriage, the only thing we did as a couple was to sink the final nails in the coffin of our relationship. From the one-sided career decisions to the choice to adopt from a foreign country, and all the little choices in between, we were each waiting for something, anything to change. But neither of us were willing to take the first step.

Overall, at least in the battle for George's well-being, I had won. So why did I feel so dreadful?

This Thanksgiving, more than any other, became about how much wine I could drink. The wine had become part of my personality and spoke for me. I drank from vengeance—to prove my angst, and to inflict guilt on my husband for the lack of his or his family's support.

The wine had a mind of its own, and I followed where it led. I drank because I felt lost. I drank to forget the man to whom I was married. But mostly, I drank to dull the pain, the anger, the guilt, and the loneliness.

Later at my in-laws', while the others corralled a mountain of dirty dishes, chatting about the Black Friday shopping they were all looking forward to, George busied himself with everyone's cell phone.

I poured myself another glass and settled into the family room, no longer caring about anyone's opinion of me. But it was more than that. I wanted them to despise me, to feel the hatred that had been building inside me for the last nine years they had lived in denial.

With every sip I took, every sidelong glance from the people in the other room, the mutual hatred, which had no words and needed none, grew.

I drank, waiting for it all to be over.

And, finally, it was.

It was only 5 pm, but my shoulders were heavy and my eyes bleary. George had been picked up and taken back to the group home. Thanksgiving dinner was over and cleaned up. I left the Thomases in silence; I didn't have to dodge hugs and kisses. None were directed my way.

CHAPTER 1
THE OLDEST PROFESSION

I can fix anything. I am Mother. The lioness with her cub. Hear me roar.

Growing up in an Italian family, I was taught that motherhood was the greatest thing a woman could do with her life. Mothers can fix anything.

And motherhood meant food. Great food. Food that puts you on the floor. No matter what's eating you, you're eating gravy, what real Italians call tomato sauce, and by the time you're done, you're so stuffed you can't breathe, so you can't remember what had been eating you in the first place.

That's what I remember about growing up Italian. My mother. She made the best tomato sauce in the world. I remember waking up on Sunday mornings to the smell of meatballs, redolent of garlic and olive oil, frying on the stove; the tomato sauce gurgling in a ten-gallon pot, basil and freshly grated parmesan cheese floating on the surface.

My father would come in from Del Prete's, the bakery in Bridgeport that made the best Italian bread. We called them grinders, but they were more like torpedo rolls, crunchy on both ends and so airy that they were almost empty in the middle.

While I was supposed to be getting ready for Mass, my mother would be in the shower. I knew when to strike. I had ten minutes, give or take. By the time she wiggled herself into her girdle and put on her housecoat, I would be up to my elbows in that pot. A meatball on the side if I could swing it, but I could always manage to tear off an end of the still-warm

1

bread and dunk it into the steaming red saucepan of heaven. It burned my mouth, but it was worth it.

"Get out of my gravy!" she would scream.

"It's sauce, Ma. We're in America. Sauce. Get with it."

Whether we had a houseful of company, or it was just the three of us, that's how every Sunday went until my father died, when I was only sixteen. Oy.

My sister Emily, who is almost fourteen years older than me, was married when I turned six. So, most Sundays it was just the three of us, and whoever else might come by. My father came from a large family; his six brothers and two sisters and their families all lived within an hour's drive, so you never knew—they could come over. My mother always cooked like she expected them to be there.

And when they did come, it was raucous. Loud, messy, and fun. The total opposite of the rest of my mother's well-ordered week.

Uncle Johnny, my favorite, would stick out his tongue at me when he came in the door. In his singsong voice, he would say "B-r-a-t, B-r-a-t, B-r-a-t, Brat Brat Brat." He always got me in trouble because my father would round the corner just as I was sticking my tongue back out at him.

Uncle Pete would bring me fruit baskets, big ones, the kind you send to people's homes when somebody dies. I would eat all the fruit, all by myself. Don't ask me how I don't weigh three hundred pounds.

Uncle Bobo thought he was talented, especially after several scotch and sodas, and he would sing original tunes about how great his kids were, songs he was probably composing as he went, because we never heard the same song twice. He would accompany himself on the guitar with the few chords he knew. His daughter Laurelle and I would dress up our Chihuahuas and put on skits for the family. Her dog always got to be the bride, since the doll clothes fit her, so my Lassie had to be the groom, even though she was a girl. Our big finish was a dance routine, sometimes the Hokey Pokey.

Nonno, my father's father, would sit at our kitchen table and sing "O Sole Mio," a cappella, drawing on his cigar between verses, at over ninety years old.

After everyone was in a food coma, all the jokes had been told, maybe a game of cards, it would be time for me to play the piano. I loved an audience just as much as the rest of them. The crazy wonderful thing about the Ferraros is, we all thought we were famous; we just hadn't been discovered yet.

Yes, motherhood was what life for an Italian woman was all about. But to succeed as a respectable Italian mother, first, you have to have a husband.

CHAPTER 2
THE FAMILIES

I met the man I would marry during my first year of law school. Joe was in his third year, and about to graduate. It took him two years to propose; he waited until he had his first job before we got engaged. I was getting a little nervous that it would never happen. What if I left law school without a husband? After all, when again would I ever be surrounded by so many available, nice looking men?

Even though I had been around Joe's parents several times, I didn't know them very well. But I knew enough about them to be afraid to expose his family to mine. I was scared that my mother would embarrass me in front of my rather conservative in-laws-to-be. They weren't like us. I wanted them to approve of me. In my family, we screamed at each other, cursed in Italian vulgarities so crude they would make a truck driver blush, and we threw things, sometimes making contact. So far all I had seen Joe's family do was smile and nod and titter, that nervous little laugh that's more a sneeze than a guffaw.

Once Joe and I decided to make our relationship official, I was out of excuses to keep our families apart. My mother already liked Joe. She figured he was my last chance at marriage. He wasn't Italian, but Lebanese Catholic was as close as I could get to my mother's vision of a proper son-in-law.

My mother was getting nervous, too. At this rate, I would be thirty before we got married, and that would make me an *older bride*.

Joe came from a good family, by all standards. The Thomases were well-known and respected in the community. Joe was dark-haired and swarthy, and with those broad shoulders and puppy-dog eyes, he could pass for a *paisano*. He was soft-spoken, well-dressed, and about to graduate from law school. When he pretended to enjoy my mother's Italian cheese pie, the deal was sealed, as far as my mother was concerned. (It would be years before my mother learned that Joe hated cheese pie.)

My mother Louise invited the Thomases for Sunday dinner, so we could get to know each other.

Muriel, my future mother-in-law, arrived in a soft pink St. John knit pantsuit, hair perfectly coiffed, every strand sprayed into submission. Her designer pumps matched her bag. Her husband Joseph was tall, his gray suit perfectly pressed, white dress shirt with a silk tie. I wondered where they were going after this and whether they'd brought bibs or a change of clothes. They probably didn't know many Italian people because they certainly weren't dressed for tomato sauce.

We greeted them at the door, my mother coming forward for hugs, still in her housedress and apron. When Muriel held out a pink chiffon cake with her left hand and her right for a handshake, I knew the Thomas family was in for a shock to their systems.

The table was set for nine. My sister and her husband had driven in from Waterbury with their three children. We had to put the leaf in the table to make it long enough for all of us to sit together in the dining room. My mother used the good china she only allowed out of the break-front for special occasions, along with the crystal, and the silver that had to be polished, of course, because we never used it. Setting the table for this meal had been a two-day affair. When we were done, the dining room looked like Don Corleone was coming.

Joe thought he was done at the pasta course. He'd already had anti-pasto and a Manhattan while we were all crouched together on the cut velvet sofa that occupied the living room. Thank God my mother at least stopped short of covering the sofa in plastic, like Aunt Tessie did. When we went to Aunt Tessie's house, we always came back with sweaty thighs.

Italians made charcuterie cool before it was a thing, and we spiced it up with prosciutto and salami. And we served it with class. On silver trays, set on the marble-topped coffee table.

When we finally sat down to dinner, there was wedding soup, with the little handmade meatballs floating in broth, surrounded by the tiny pasta we called *acini di pepe*, and escarole. Then, lasagna.

And of course, the wine flowed. Smiling demurely, Joe's parents accepted one glass each and declined more. We each had three . . . or so.

As the meatballs came out of the gravy and a roast chicken was placed on the table, Joe's eyes widened. I think it was fear. He whispered to me, "There's more?"

I just smiled and passed him the chunky, oily, garlicky, oregano-baked-with-the-chicken vegetables, along with the extra gravy. And by gravy, I mean sauce. My mother's famous red deliciousness. What are you going to dip the Italian bread in if you don't have extra gravy?

Tossed salad came next, dressed in the extra virgin olive oil my mother bought by the gallon from Frosinone, the Italian import store, and vinegar from our wine cellar.

"It will help you digest," my mother instructed.

With his own hands, my grandfather, my mother's father, had built us a wine cellar, which served as the foundation for the back deck he also built for us, an addition to the ranch home in which I grew up. In the wine cellar were several casks, two holding my grandfather's home-brewed table wine. The third was reserved as the vinegar barrel. In it went any wine we ever opened that went bad. Until my mother sold that house, we had the best vinegar in the neighborhood.

Madonna mia, could my mother cook.

"Now," I told Joe, "we're done."

I lied. What I meant was, "Now you can take a break."

Growing up it was always my job to clear the table while the "grown-ups" talked. Today was no different. My mother would load the dishwasher, issuing instructions over her shoulder as she did.

"Get the pastries and put them on that platter."

Luigi's Bakery made the best, and we had at least a dozen miniature cannoli, eclairs, and *sfogliatelle*, the flaky crunchy pieces of heaven stuffed with cream. Just like we used to do every Sunday while my father was alive, just in case somebody came over.

Fresh cantaloupe, espresso with Sambuca, the licorice-flavored liqueur that made every coffee better, and maybe some torrone, the Italian nougat candy that was a staple in every Italian American household. And now, you've got dessert.

In true Louise style, food in our house was served from introductions to goodbyes. And sometimes leftovers followed guests out the door.

Satisfied that her son would at least eat well, Joe's mother approved of me. And if Muriel approved, so did the rest of the Thomas clan.

The Thomases assumed that I got my culinary skills from my mother. I didn't, but I did get something from her. When Joe and I got married and I had resigned myself to the fact that I was cooking dinner every night, my husband would come home to pot after pot of some weird concoction I had thrown together. Growing up, my nose was always in books while my sister was learning to cook at my mother's knee. Cooking for me wasn't as instinctive as I hoped it would be. Somehow, when my mother threw random ingredients in a pot, something delicious emerged. Not so much for me.

But something stuck. I always made way too much.

"Who's coming?" Joe would ask.

"You never know, somebody could come, and then we wouldn't have enough" was the answer he always got.

Nobody ever came, but at least I was ready.

CHAPTER 3
THE NOD

There was a hole in my soul. But I had a plan to fill it. All I needed was for Joe to start nodding. That was what our decision-making as a couple had become: the tacit approval of the other when it became apparent that no mutual decision could be reached.

It started innocently enough, as most cracks in marriages do. A slight disagreement, a compromise which seemed small at the time, until that gap turns into a gaping cleft in the earth that swallows everything in its path.

We had been married for a week, two lawyers who met at a prestigious Connecticut law school. We had taken a honeymoon designed for the couple we thought we would become. I was spoiled from seven straight days of room service, umbrella drinks served on the beach at the rise of the little white flag. Every morning, fresh flowers were strewn in the private pool of our suite, by Pepe or Miguel.

The argument started over whether to have dinner in or go out.

"You know," Joe said, "we just got home from eating out every night. We can't spend the money."

I countered with "I'm too tired to cook. You do it, then."

When Joe picked up the house phone, I thought he was ordering takeout. Even though Joe had been calling his mom every day from our honeymoon, asking his mother's advice while we were in the midst of a disagreement was the last thing I expected.

I exploded. "Put that phone down or I'm out of here."

The phone landed in the cradle a few moments too late to mollify me.

I chose the closest weapon in my armament. The tomato whizzed by his ear and smacked into the wall, suspended there for a millisecond. Juice flowed in crimson watercolor drips, and, in slow motion, the tomato slid to the floor.

Joe stood up, flat expression on his face, and went to fetch the paper towels. He did not utter a word, just conducted the cleanup as best he could. The shadow of that tomato remained on the wall for years after it was thrown, a bitter reminder that I could not start a good fight, or even a decent screaming match.

I swallowed my nagging dissatisfaction in favor of a pretense of harmony. Something was starting to eat at me, but I couldn't put my finger on its exact source.

Three years into our marriage, Joe came home from the office with big news. He had been working for a two-attorney firm, a move I had begged him not to make.

"A larger firm would be better. We need benefits. You know, health insurance, pension, security." I told him all this, but he would hear none of it. I believed that he had consulted with his parents and made this decision before he discussed it with me, but I fought that voice in my head.

Joe continued. "I am going out on my own. I am going to open my own practice."

I would not be quieted. "No. We can't afford it."

He went ahead with his plans anyway, setting up shop in the very office in which he had been employed, except now there would be no paycheck. He had to bring in his own clients and pay rent. As if to mock me, he was still bringing home orange dust in the cuffs of his dress trousers, a reminder of the shag carpet that lined the floor of his office.

Everything was original from the time the building had been constructed in the 1970s, down to the dull brown paneled walls and suspended ceilings. On a good day, you could hear the fluorescent bulbs crackling in time with the other lights that hung overhead, struggling to share the yellow cast for which they were famed.

At the same time Joe was making his plans to go entrepreneurial, I was let go from my first job as a practicing attorney. My boss called me into his office. He blamed the economy. Business was slow. But I knew the real reason for my dismissal. The manager of the firm was not a lawyer, but she had authority over me. She also was having a very personal relationship with my married boss. She relished telling me how to run the files. One day, my manager Maureen ordered me to have a private conversation, in chambers, with the judge on one of our cases, without opposing counsel present. She wanted me to discuss the merits of our motion and attempt to persuade the judge to rule in our favor. When I quoted her the specific ethics rule that prohibited me from doing as she asked, Maureen decided she wanted me gone. And that was the day I got fired.

I was also pregnant with our first child.

Practicing law was okay. It wasn't as exciting as law school, where the fact patterns were exaggerated and the outcomes didn't matter, because it was all hypothetical. In the real world, you had to sit through depositions where your client listed every piece of underwear they lost in the fire, or what the guy behind him was wearing when he ran into your client with his car, and it was all under oath.

Now that I was growing an actual human being inside my body, I felt like I was doing something that mattered in the world. I knew, but kept the knowledge to myself, that I would not be anxious to go back to work once I gave birth. I didn't want to hire a nanny, either. No way would I let someone else raise my child.

Joe pounced on the opportunity to say "I need your help in the office."

I had no valid objections; after all, I was available during the day now. For a few months, I let Joe labor under the pretense that I was happy to be helping out in his practice. It was no small feat for four attorneys to share a three-person office. There were now two separate law practices, still sharing the space of one practice. It got tricky. When Joe was not with clients, my files and I occupied the visitor side of his massive desk. When he was, I was relegated to the conference room. When both spots were full, I would hope that one of the secretaries was out to lunch so that I could sit in her cubicle for an hour. If not, I roamed the hall, files in my arms, until a spot opened up.

When my husband rewrote my briefs, I bristled. All the while, I allowed him to trudge through the extra work he had created for himself. When he stood over my shoulder, amending the motions I constructed with workmanlike precision, I rolled my eyes at the computer screen. I got lots of practice pretending to listen to the corrections he issued. My legal writing skills, which were top of the class in law school, failed to meet his standards, and he let me know.

As my belly swelled, my patience shrank.

Two weeks before the birth, during some dissatisfaction over a client letter I had written, Joe fired me. He was on my last nerve, and I was waiting for an excuse to get out of there anyway. Car keys in hand, I made for the door.

To add insult to the firing, Joe didn't even notice I was gone until my waiter had set down my chef's salad. When my cell phone rang, I answered calmly.

"Where did you go?" he asked.

"You fired me, remember?"

"You actually left? What time will you be back?"

I let the question hang, finished the call—and my lunch—and drove to the mall.

Our son was born four years after Joe and I married, on August 10th, his daddy's birthday. Adding to the confusion of having two Josephs in the house, they also shared a birth date. My father-in-law was also a Joseph, so that made three. It would have been easier if they each had a nickname, to avoid confusion. The closest we ever got to nicknames was to use varying degrees of formality: Joseph, Joe and Joey. When they were all together and you called one of them, either Joseph (the elder), Joe (my husband) or Joey (my son), either everybody answered, or no one.

That's not what was supposed to happen. My son's name was supposed to be Matthew. I had been through the back of the Bible, the part where Christian names are listed and decoded. I felt that a name which meant "gift from God" was appropriate for our first son. My husband had been nodding the whole time I chattered on about the significance of such a name. Wasn't it wonderful that there was actually a name for our child which expressed how we felt?

When I first held my sweet baby in my arms, I said "Welcome, Matthew."

As he took his first suckle from my breast, I said, "Are you hungry, Matthew?"

When I changed his diaper for the first time, I cooed at my little Matthew.

For the three days it took me to recover from the cesarean birth, Joe never uttered that name, just held our son in his arms. He remained silent while I introduced him to visitors with "Meet my little Matthew." When Social Services came into my hospital room to fill out our son's birth certificate, I said "His name is Matthew."

Muriel's large hazel eyes widened to their full measure and met mine. My mother-in-law, the doyenne of my husband's large Middle Eastern family, was visiting, at a moment of such importance to me. Those eyes could mean excitement, hatred, anger, surprise. I've always had trouble reading people with hazel eyes, and my mother-in-law was no exception. When my mother was angry, her brown eyes turned dark and murky. When my best high school friend's blue eyes got deep like the ocean, I knew that Bonnie was sad. But hazel eyes don't give you advance notice. The only clue I had as to what was coming was that her pre-Parkinson's head was now in full shake. And her lips were clamped. The temperature in the room dropped twenty degrees. In that split second, kindly doting turned to indignation.

"Actually," Joe said from the chair next to my bed, "his name is Joseph Matthew." My husband rose to his full six-foot frame and shot me a warning glance that could only mean, "Do not cross my mother."

Even though I wanted to scream at Muriel, my mother's mantra "Wives are submissive to their husbands" was playing in my head. Besides, Muriel scared me just a little. Before I got pregnant, she was always taking me to lunch, asking me why we had yet to present her with a grandchild. Okay, she scared me a lot.

I was one-two punched. Instead of protesting, I threw my head to the side and hid the tears which revealed my humiliation and disappointment. I signed the birth certificate declaring my son's name to be Joseph Matthew.

My husband was the firstborn in his family, an only son. He was followed by three girls, the sisters who waited on him, fulfilled his every wish before he was even aware of it. They had been named alliteratively … all three of the names of Joe's sisters began with the letter "L". Convenient. Joe didn't even have to complete a sentence before being waited on. "Could I have a glass of water La…" was as far as he had to go. Joe had earned the nickname "Prince Khalil" in college. I guess his friends called Joe by his middle name because it sounded more exotic, more regal… more spoiled. Whenever he would bring his roommates home for dinner, his buddies would be treated to the sight of one of Joe's three sisters jumping up from the table to refill his iced tea. Or fetch him another napkin. Or a cookie.

The *New York Times Magazine* had just run a story about the Birkin bags women on the Upper East Side of Manhattan had been gifted upon presenting their husbands with their first sons. I had given Prince Joe the first boy to carry on the Thomas name. An heir to the throne requires a present of magnitude. I knew the Birkin bag was out of the question, but let myself wonder what delightful trinket Joe would dream up to thank me for his own little prince.

Instead, once the social worker was gone, Joe handed me three manila files.

"Here," he said, "I need you to look these over. There are a couple of letters you need to sign, and I need to get them out right away. When do you think you will be back in the office?"

I silently vowed not to be bulldozed again.

We began making one-sided decisions. Joe had been making all the big decisions with the advice and consent of his parents, mainly his mom. She believed that there was more prestige in owning one's own law firm than having the security of a nice, reliable paycheck and a 401(k). So that's exactly what Joe did. When one of the partners was elevated to the bench and traded his practice of law for black robes, he had no need for his office and offered it to Joe. In a short time, Joe went from renting his former office from his ex-bosses to buying half the office building.

The second partner died five years later. Over my earnest protests, but with the encouragement of his family, Joe committed to buying the other half of the office building from the attorney's widow. I lost this argument before I'd even opened my mouth. My opinion had not been heard for so long that it was futile to even express my opinion.

I decided to join in the fun. In my own little way, I secretly started taking back control, one little spending spree at a time. I became a decision-making, money-spending monster. No major purchases at any one time, just small acts of revenge for partnership lost. If I had checks in my checkbook, I had money. There was no more asking for cash for groceries. I just went to the store and wrote a check. Baby needs shoes? Macy's charge card was ever at the ready. Going to a party? A new dress was in my future. We took vacations we could not afford, at my insistence.

I made excuse after excuse for not going to the office. Doctors' appointments. Play dates. One of us was not feeling well. Joey might take his first step today, or cut a tooth, or he might even be running a fever. On the rare occasion that I found myself without pretext, I would drag myself into the wood-paneled, shag-carpeted building that was Joe's empire.

But I was always sure to come up with some ingredient lacking for dinner. Failing that, I would need to run to the mall for some emergency piece of clothing or pair of shoes. Being everything to everyone was exhausting, and always required me to make my exit after an hour or two. I justified my absence by telling myself *I refuse to shovel into the financial abyss that Joe created, with his mother's blessing.*

In the midst of this, however, I failed to take responsibility for the financial storm that I had brewing. I justified my frequent purchases by keeping them low, twenty or forty dollars at a time. The bills began to roll in, but Joe never commented or complained. He seemed to know that he had taken my power, and this was all I had left.

Soon I recognized the source of the hole in my soul. As hard as I tried, I couldn't shop it full, drink it full, or nag it full. Joey had finished kindergarten, and there went my excuse that I could not possibly get to the office, work on files, and get back to pick up my son in three hours. Joey was now ready to take on first grade. A full day of school.

A second child was called for.

We had been making halfhearted attempts at trying to conceive naturally. Our physical relationship had become a chore for me, and I was happiest when our encounters were over. My declining respect for Joe, and the knowledge that I was only being paid lip service, affected my desire for him. Having to remember that the end goal was another child was the only thing that got me into his bed.

After a couple of years of the natural method, we sought the help of fertility specialists. The final straw of the scientific approach came, for me, one Saturday morning about six months into the process. Reaching my fortieth birthday also meant the end of the line for in vitro fertilization. If this did not work, we would have to consider surrogacy. We were religious about the injections which were supposedly providing my eggs with the fountain of youth. The mornings came when I was matter-of-factly told that I was ovulating, and Joe performed the requisite look-at-porn-and-cum-in-the-vial procedure for me to take to the clinic.

I had been poked and prodded over and over by the doctors on this team, most of them women, all of them hell-bent on impregnating me. On the morning of my final impregnation attempt, I was lying on the examining room table, waiting for Joe's sperm to be whipped into a frenzy of fertility, my legs in stirrups, a home decorating magazine held in the air over my head. A knock at the door, and in strode the definition of the well-dressed man: tie in a perfect Windsor knot, the fine weave of his pinpoint cotton shirt fitted to his trim and well-toned torso, not a strand of his dark hair out of place, piercing blue eyes, holding something resembling a turkey baster in his free hand. He said, "Hello. I'm Dr. Antoun. Please relax."

The idea of this handsome stranger ready to shoot me with sperm, without so much as a little small talk, threw me into a full fit of laughter, complete with stomach spasms, all the while making my eyelashes flutter, my face flush. As I propped myself up on my elbows, I managed to spit out, "What? No flowers? No music? No candlelight?"

The in vitro did not work, and having aged out of the process, it was no longer an option for me.

Reviewing the candidates for surrogacy was an exercise in culture shock. The objectionable questions came rapid-fire. "Would you accept a surrogate who has smoked marijuana?" "Would you accept a recovering alcoholic to carry your baby?" "Do you require her to have a college education?" "There could be some unforeseen complications for which you would also be responsible. Are you aware of that?" "Are you prepared to pay for all of her medical expenses out of pocket?"

Joey was three when we purchased our five-bedroom colonial in the suburbs. We couldn't afford it, but we had outgrown our townhouse. It simply couldn't hold all the toys and equipment we felt we needed for our little family.

The new house had been the model home for the development, and came with all kinds of perks, like custom decorating and upgrades. The middle bedroom was decorated in a nursery theme. Little pink bears danced along the cream walls, and the made-to-order draperies had pink balloons in the same bubble-gum shade as the bears. I took it as a sign that I would have the little girl I always knew I would have. Her name would be Caroline, a tribute to my maternal grandmother, who suffered unspeakable violence at the hands of my grandfather. They had traveled to the United States together as teenage newlyweds, from the back woods of the Frosinone district of Italy. It was not a place known for its cultural finesse, its only claim to fame that it was the birthplace of St. Thomas Aquinas. At the time my grandparents left the little town of Roccasecca, it was known for its thievery. Neither one of them spoke English, and up until the day she died, my grandmother could not read. To my grandfather, she was chattel, mere property, and I sought a way to pay homage to her suffering.

The little pink nursery became my refuge. Throughout the fertility process, I had developed a self-soothing habit. Every morning after Joe left for the office, I would sit in the softly padded rocking chair that I had placed in the corner of the room. It sat there in expectation of the inevitable baby girl who would occupy that room. Rocking there, drinking coffee, and sobbing softly into the sleeve of my plush terry robe somehow allayed the indignities of the past couple of years. Being poked and prodded on the metal table with the stirrups, having sex by appointment, and, finally, considering surrogacy would all be worth it once Caroline was in my arms. Thinking of holding my baby girl, in that chair, made all of it bearable.

It was the morning of my fortieth birthday. This was the last day I would be eligible for in vitro. My eggs were now officially too old to fertilize.

As Joe went out the door, he threw the promise of a special dinner over his shoulder. I knew it would not take place. My birthdays had become an inconvenience for him. My demands on his time were a debt to pay if he came home from the office early enough. I knew that he would find himself too busy to leave the office at a decent hour. We would end up eating Chinese takeout on the sofa, followed by a grocery store birthday cake purchased as an afterthought on his way home.

I started my usual morning routine; steaming mug in hand, I made my way up the stairs to my perch. My steps were heavier than usual, sadness laden with finality. One more door closing.

As if in slow motion, the mug flew out of my hand. I could only watch as the floating bears, the baby blue carpeting, and the balloons were coated in a wash of brown.

As I was scrubbing the walls and the carpet and spot-cleaning the draperies, a feeling of calm overcame me. I said aloud, seemingly to the ceiling, "Okay, I get it."

I shut the door behind me, filled with a feeling of faith—no, knowledge. I knew that I would never again sit in that rocker in desperate anticipation. I believed that the coffee flying everywhere was a sign that I should get out of God's way—that the little girl I'd been dreaming of would be sleeping in that bedroom soon. I didn't know how it would happen; I just knew it would. Apparently, faith comes at the expense of reason.

That evening progressed as anticipated. Joe was collapsed on the sofa in the family room, the ever-present remote in his hand. He flipped through channels faster than I could register the programs, let alone decide whether I wanted to watch. The remnants of a halfhearted celebration were strewn on the coffee table. The remainder of a stale vanilla cake (my favorite is chocolate blackout), which originally read *Happy Birthday Mommy*, but now with three pieces cut out, read *Hap Birth Mo*. Beside it sat half-empty containers of kung pao chicken, chopsticks askew, sticking out of the boxes like wooden antennas. The dregs of a bottle of champagne were all that remained of my fortieth birthday present to myself.

My son Joey, a chubby six-year-old with my heart in his hand, proudly presented me with a gift, and climbed into my lap while I opened it. My little boy was as surprised by the contents as I was. A necklace from the local jeweler. Another stop on the way home from the office, no doubt. A thin gold chain with a little gold squiggle and the tiniest suggestion of a diamond emerged from the box. The little gold squiggle reminded me of sperm.

Only that morning, my pregnancy attempt had been defeated by science. And now, even the gift seemed to be mocking my inability to conceive.

Despite the heaviness of the meal and the sugar, I finally got my little boy to sleep. It was too early to turn in myself without starting an argument with Joe. Even though he didn't care whether I wanted to watch the programs he liked, he wanted me to sit there with him. I begrudgingly returned to the sofa where Joe was still engrossed in speed-channel-surfing.

I was feeling caged, desperate, and trapped. So when Joe threw out a comment, eyes still glued to the screen—"You know, I could really use your help in the office tomorrow"—I fought the urge to snap.

Instead, I said, "You know, Sharon's sister works for an adoption agency. An international one, at that. We would never have to see the birth mother or have any contact with her."

Sharon had been my best friend since college. When she married a man from Florida and moved there to be with him, Sharon and I made a plan to relocate my family so that we could all be together. I trusted the information she gave me, perhaps a little too much.

"No," the retort came instantly, "I won't do it. If it's not my child, I don't want it."

But that was okay. I'd expected that answer. I had planted the seed. And that was good enough for now.

Motherhood was the one thing I considered myself adept at; I knew I wanted more of it. All I needed to do was nag Joe long enough for him to nod in the general direction of yes. It only took me about two weeks (I had gotten really good at nagging him into compliance). Joe figured that if he agreed to do whatever I wanted, he didn't actually have to follow through; at the very least, it would shut me up.

I don't think he ever expected that I had a plan for him to make good on this one.

This time, as with all the others, he nodded. And once he did, I was off. The wheels were in motion before he could think twice about what he had just agreed to do.

We chose our adoption agency for two reasons: My friend Sharon had recommended it, and they had the name "Christian" in the title. Their website had pictures of happy families, complete with heartwarming stories of how children from all over the world came to the United States to find their forever homes. Families at play together, dads with toddlers riding on their shoulders. The testimonials were glowing, written by grateful adoptive parents who were happy and proud of their new children, their families complete.

Finding no reason not to choose this agency, we looked no further, confident that we were in good hands with an outfit we could trust to find our little Caroline, wherever she might be, and deliver her to us.

I had just enough credit on the Visa card for the $5,000 deposit to get the ball rolling. Never mind that the total cost of the international adoption was the equivalent of a king's ransom. Before we were done, we would spend more than $25,000. The costs were in the materials from our adoption agency, but I didn't show them to my husband. Joe didn't need that piece of information just yet. Reading the numbers from the card to the adoption agent, I felt a power I had not felt since the day my acceptance letter to law school had come in the mail. Funds were transferred. There was no turning back.

As long as we passed the home study, we were well on our way toward becoming parents to my little Caroline.

CHAPTER 4
LOGIC IS RELATIVE

A few months later, we found ourselves facing Sister Mary Louise and her interrogation, delivered on behalf of Catholic Charities, our home study provider.

The rotund nun struggled to make herself comfortable on our formal living room sofa, the glass-topped coffee table too close to her puffy knees. I fidgeted with the tea and cookies that were trembling in time with the shaking of my hands. As I set the tray down, she asked, "What would happen if the child you adopt turns out to have a disability?"

It was a question I had not allowed myself to ponder. Without missing a beat, Joe answered, "I am not prepared to parent a handicapped child."

The cup in my hand landed with a jangle. Tea spilled everywhere. The nearby paperwork that was to determine the future of our parenting was saved in the nick of time.

As the shock of his answer hit me, I shot him the death stare, yet he continued. "I suppose, if it happened, I would deal with it. But I am not emotionally prepared to parent a child with challenges."

This was the final hurdle in the quest for the child who would salvage my life's purpose. And he was screwing it up.

As if that weren't enough of a shock to my system, Sister Mary Louise wanted to know more. "Why won't you consider adopting domestically?" she asked. "You know, there are lots of American children who need homes. And, oh, by the way, did you know that you can have picnics with the birth mother?"

Instead of saying "Over my cold, lifeless body. No way will someone knock on my door and say, 'May I take little Caroline to the mall?,'" I explained my background as a family lawyer. I told her about my experience with the trend in the law toward open domestic adoptions. I described how having a birth mother appear on my doorstep unannounced was unappealing and unacceptable to me. International adoption seemed the perfect solution.

After what seemed like three days but turned out to be just short of an hour, the interview was over. The final portion of the home study consisted of a quick tour of the two stories that would comprise our child's new home. I kept a neat house, but not obsessively so. The memory of my mother's incessant cleaning before we could have any fun made me determined not to be that kind of mother. Throughout my childhood, whenever my mother and I left the house, she made us back out the door. Even when we were leaving for something really fun, like going to New York for a Broadway show, the house had to be pristine—"So we wouldn't come back to a mess."

Whenever my mother was visiting my house, she would walk around, gathering everything that even looked fragile from the coffee tables, arranging them in the glass-enclosed breakfront in my dining room, "so they wouldn't break."

It always took me a couple of hours after she left to rearrange my home, mumbling under my breath, *I don't live in a museum, Mom.*

Inspecting the two acres out back where our child would play, and the room that would be our new child's bedroom, Sister Mary Louise clucked and nodded in approval.

As the door shut behind her, I held my breath, waiting for the plump nun to negotiate her way down the steps of the front porch. The flaps of her wimple flew away from her head like butterfly wings attempting to lift an eagle. I sucked in my breath as she struggled down the cobblestone walkway to the driveway. I watched as she hefted herself into the tiny Toyota which could not have been chosen for her comfort.

Certain that she was finally out of earshot, I let out a low, guttural moan, so pained that I was shocked and surprised by the depth of the wail. My chest broke out into an itchy, angry rash that I had never experienced before.

Turning toward Joe, I screamed at the top of my lungs, "How could you say that? How could you tell her you couldn't have a handicapped child? How could you do that to me? We'll never get approved now."

I wished at that moment to have a knife, a sharp one, in my hand, to cut his heart out and serve it up on the very tray that was holding the remnants of the Milano-cookies-for-the-meeting-with-the-nun.

With his ever-present and unnerving cool, Joe said, "I was just being honest."

Gotta give him that one. At least he was being honest.

As I rifled through the medicine cabinet for a salve for this sudden outbreak of hives, I was left with the echo of Sister Mary Louise's last insightful question. *Why did I feel the urgent need to adopt a child?*

I had no legitimate answer, but a canned one at the ready. "We have a lot of love to give another child. Our son needs a sibling."

But what was the real truth here? Was it that my son Joey was away too many hours of the day to justify my staying out of the office? Did I hate my profession so much that I could not bear to practice law? Or was it that I did not want to be censored by my husband, my law partner, and ostensible life partner? He walked all over everything that touched my life. Even when we were out for social occasions, he would cringe when I opened my mouth to tell a joke, to relate a story, to throw my head back for a hearty laugh. Later, it would always be "I wouldn't have said that if I were you."

Had I been suffocating since the first day he'd said "I need your help in the office?"

Did it take a week, a month, or a year to realize that I had no autonomy in any aspect of my life? Was this how I planned to reinvent myself—with another project over which I had at least some control? Was my life this empty?

The questions swirled, but I didn't allow myself to entertain the answers. I was focused simply on the task at hand. I had tunnel vision: Get past this interview, and be approved.

Yes, approval was my goal. I needed someone to stamp *worthy* on my forehead. Yes, even if it was for the continuation of my being needed for motherhood, or what I perceived it to be. Was it my excuse to stay at home a few more years? What did motherhood mean to me then? A doting caregiver, someone who could be relied upon to sustain the life of someone dependent on me? I needed someone who would look up at me with grateful eyes. I needed someone to hold me on a pedestal as all-knowing, all-caring, and all-powerful.

Who, exactly, did I think I was? Nobody and everybody. Was I was so lacking in self-confidence that I needed to prop myself up with a feeling of importance, the need to mean the whole world to someone? I wasn't getting it from my husband, the man who consulted his mother on every major decision, or to ask her to settle every one of our marital disagreements. Nor was I getting it from my six-year-old son Joey, who seemed like such an old soul that he was raising me.

I was needy, lacking, and looking for an escape from the office where Joe, my husband and law partner, held court. Where he would dictate which files he needed worked on, whether it was an area of law I was interested in practicing or not. Where the debts were piling up. Where we were lucky to make enough every month to pay the mortgage on a house in which we had no business living. The debt grew daily, yet I could not bring myself to walk into that office. I felt it was a hopeless, bottomless pit, and I refused to participate.

But that was not how it all started. There was a time when I'd looked forward to a future with Joe.

Joe and I weren't exactly introduced to each other in law school. We were described to each other by a mutual classmate. When she described me to Joe, she said, "Look for *Nastassja Kinski*." I guess that was a compliment, although my mother was convinced that I looked like Sophia Loren, one of the few flattering remarks she ever threw my way.

My mother could only express her approval of me if it reflected back on her. Since we had such a strong resemblance to each other, she could afford the praise; she was really paying tribute to her own good looks.

When Joe finally approached me, in his red shirt, a requisite for the Valentine's Day house party we were both attending, his opening line was: "Aren't you Nancy? I think I wanted to meet you."

My first thoughts were, *Does he know I'm on a date—with another guy?* Followed by *Wanted to meet me? Does he still? What a loser.*

But the broad shoulders, dark hairy chest, and the brown eyes that drooped just a little at the corners, making him look just a little bit sad, kept me there a minute longer than I'd intended. The glowing endorsement from my friend kept me planted longer than my date would have preferred.

We got past the initial discomfort with my nervous giggle, a people-pleasing technique I had adopted as a teenager, to put boys at ease. This habit followed me into adulthood. Since it worked, I used it to my advantage, or so I thought. If I had an ounce of fortitude, I would have—should have—said, "When you figure it out, let me know." I should have turned on my heel and returned to my date. Dan, my escort that evening, was a fellow law student, curly-haired and gawky. But he made up for his lack of looks and social graces with his excellent singing voice and penchant for serenading me with Frank Sinatra tunes.

But I did not speak up. I allowed Joe to corner me for what seemed like a few minutes but was apparently long enough to annoy Dan, across the room.

Joe and I chatted and laughed about nonsense, and gossiped about our professors. He told me which ones to avoid and how to get an A in Torts. Finally, the volume of beer got to him, and Joe had to excuse himself.

Out of the corner of my eye, I watched as Dan ran across the room with my coat, much the way I imagined a toreador would taunt a bull, and rushed me out of the party.

When Joe and I had our first date, we laughed about how I was gone when he returned from the restroom. I had not made a great first impression. The fact that I remembered his name when we next met was enough for him to ask me out.

After our first date, we were together every moment we were not in class. He fished me out of the bowl that was law school, a veritable candy store for a reasonably cute female law student in search of male companionship.

I didn't see it that way, and neither did my mother. I was already twenty-seven years old by the time I started studying law and living in the basement apartment of my childhood home. I was reminded daily by my Italian, Catholic mama that I was starting to resemble an old maid.

Don't you know that men don't buy the cow if they get the milk for free?

You're not getting any younger; who's going to want an old, non-virginal whore like you? Don't you think you should hurry up and choose one of these suckers before they figure that out?

These old-world Italianisms followed me around campus, from class to class, and to the "Thank Goodness It's Thursday" parties that were a traditional part of my law school life.

You might call me a late bloomer. In high school and college, I was the odd girl, a little too awkward and self-aware to enjoy attention from the opposite sex. Not that I didn't get any; I just wasn't comfortable enough in my skin to enjoy it.

By the time I entered law school, I had already moved away from—and then moved back to—my childhood home. I had lost myself, and found myself. I had failed and succeeded at a variety of meaningless jobs. Through this process, I had started liking myself a little and was feeling a bit more confident in my own skin. I was getting attention from men, lots of them, short and tall, handsome, and not so.

But the nagging little voice in the back of my head kept me from enjoying the collection of handsome male brainiacs that was law school. I became focused on finding a husband. I had forgotten that I was educating myself to power, that I could write my own ticket without a man in my life. My mother had convinced me that I was powerless without my Mrs. degree. I was convinced that I had to be Mrs. somebody to actually be somebody.

Since Joe seemed the most likely candidate to confer that degree on me, I let him follow me until he caught me.

CHAPTER 5
APPROVED FOR WHAT?

Several weeks after our interrogation by Sister Mary Louise, the report was finally in: We were cleared to be international adoptive parents; now we needed to choose a country of origin.

"Why? Just send me the first available infant girl," was my instant reaction. But apparently, there were procedures to follow, and our adoption agency wasn't about to bend the rules for us.

"You need to pick a country, Mrs. Thomas. Then we work with that country's foundation to locate a child for you."

"What are our choices?"

I bent to Joe's will on this one. After all, I had him on the hook for about twenty-five large. I guessed I could let him pick the country of origin of our next child.

He decided against China, Mexico, and Guatemala. Romania was the only choice left. Yes, they'd had their share of bad press around children who had been ignored and abused in orphanages, but Romania was striving to join the European Union. As a united front, the member countries would be a stronger economic force than they could be on their own. For an emerging country like Romania, acceptance into the EU was vital for its survival. There were news stories all over television about how Romania had cleaned up their act, most notably in the orphanages. This had been a source of disgrace for the country, and they had seemingly dealt with it.

Besides, we reasoned, Romania was once part of the Roman Empire. Since Joe's ethnic background was Lebanese and mine was Italian, it made sense that a child from Romania, more than any of the other available countries, would most likely resemble us. She would blend in with our family.

CHAPTER 6
CAROLINE . . . NOT CAROLINE

It's only three days after we charged our second $5,000 installment for baby Caroline. I'm feeling proud of myself for finishing the paperwork so quickly and progressing us down the road toward growing our family.

Driving up Route 206 to the grocery store, planning dinner the only other thing on my mind, my cell phone rings.

It's Linda, our assigned adoption agent.

"I know you requested a baby girl, but this little boy is available," she says. "He's just so cute. He's a toddler. What do you think?"

"I don't know. We'll look at him, but no promises. We have our heart set on a baby girl," I answer.

She doesn't believe me. She doesn't have to. The Cambridge Dictionary describes a visceral reaction as a response based on emotional reactions rather than on reason or thought.

A few days later, the video comes in the mail. Once I open the mailbox, the pacing commences. I wait for my husband's workday to be over. *Of all nights, Joe, please don't be late.* It takes everything in me not to pop in the video cassette before he gets home.

Eventually, he comes in and soon we're sitting in front of the television set in the family room, rapt, watching the hazel-eyed toddler, clearly still in diapers, wander around the sparsely furnished home of his Transylvanian foster family. He reacts to instructions, picks up toys and puts them down, drools a little. They call him Gheorghe, or Georgie. We have lots of kids on Joe's side of the family named George already. He will blend.

This is the moment of conception for me. I hit rewind on the tape for hours after Joe leaves the room. Forgotten is the desire for a baby girl, replaced by my new mantra. *He is mine, and he needs me.*

Before we can officially accept George, the adoption agency and my husband insist that we review the medical report. It comes in the mail, written in Romanian. Two pages of scribble, in a foreign language, signed by somebody, MD. I issue expletives to the computer, cursing at the online translation sites. The only sentence I can get the language gods to give me is the last, *Eligibile pentru adoptarea.* Eligible for adoption. That's all I need to hear, but Joe still refuses to sign the paperwork officially accepting George.

When the English version arrives more than a week later, it could have said that George was purple with three heads and I would not have believed it. But it does not. The report says "Normal, with a slight speech delay. Eligible for adoption."

Our pediatrician reviews the sparse paperwork, watches the now almost-worn-out tape of George picking up toys and putting them down, and nods in approval. "He looks normal to me."

That's enough for me. *Slight speech delay.* I think, *I can love it out of him.*

Joe is now officially defeated, out of objections. Begrudgingly, he signs the paperwork accepting George as our son. With it, he signs the authorization to charge us the third $5,000 installment, still $10,000 to go on the ransom we are paying to salvage this child from what we consider to be a backward existence.

The adoption agency has an online chat forum, where other adoptive mothers, and the occasional father, communicate with each other while waiting on their own interminable pregnancies. There had been a lot of banter about who should review the records for our prospective adoptee. I am shocked to learn that one adoptive mother had learned that the child she was considering was found to have cystic fibrosis and was not expected to live past the age of eighteen. When I learn that she rejected him in favor of a healthier child, I am both horrified and grateful—horrified by the idea of treating an adoption like shopping for a pair of shoes, and grateful that I would not have to make that decision.

That thread starts a debate among the other expectant parents about whether to have an Eastern European expert review their prospective children's records. Dr. Jane Aronson is one of the most universally recognized experts on Romanian adoptees, and she is located in New Jersey. One parent comments, "She is inordinately negative. She will tell you that every child adopted from Romania is disabled." There is a chorus of agreement online.

I decide not to share this information with Joe; instead, we will follow the advice of our pediatrician and move forward with the adoption.

One mother had learned so much Romanian that she had made cassette tapes. I order some, and they start arriving in the mail. Back and forth to school, my six-year-old and I listen and practice the mommy Romanian phrases that will help us communicate with our little foreigner. *Spălați-vă mâinile.* Wash your hands *Doriți suc?* Would you like juice? *Doare burtica ta?* Does your tummy hurt? *Te iubesc.* I love you. We even learn some nursery rhymes and songs, amusing ourselves and each other with the odd word endings and our new, secret vocabulary.

Shopping needs to commence, as I am now in full-blown nesting mode. Furniture, outfits, toys, books—they find their way into our house on an almost daily basis. The look on Joe's face grows progressively frantic.

But we need it for our little boy, I rationalize, and continue the shopping spree in earnest.

When Linda, our adoption agent, announces that she will be making a trip to Romania to visit a number of orphanages and foster homes, including George's, I pack up as many crayons and coloring books, candy, and toys as she's willing to carry, per adoptive child.

When we receive the pictures in the mail of our little boy, there is no sign of the crayons, toys, or other treats I had rushed to mail, just a face full of chocolate and a big grin.

I gaze at this small boy in overalls, his hazel eyes huge with pleasure, enjoying what is probably his first taste of Western sweets. He is standing in a dirt courtyard, chickens running loose in the background. A cow, ribs sticking out of its sides, is attempting to graze on the only patch of grass visible in the picture, a few die-hard, sickly brown blades, sticking out of the dirt.

My heart longs to reach through the abyss, into the picture, to rescue this innocent and bring him home, to civilization, to love, to normalcy.

CHAPTER 7

GESTATION

Our trip is planned for the second week of October, nine months after we first started the adoption process. A full-term pregnancy. We would arrive in Romania just in time for George's fourth birthday, and we would give him his first American celebration. All seems to be in order, until our adoption agency calls. There's a small glitch. "Your paperwork has not been signed by the foundation yet, and it cannot be submitted to the court until it has. There are rumors of Romanian children being adopted into the United States to be used for medical experimentation."

The foreign government knows that the rumors are a fraud, and so do we. But we have to wait until the powers in charge calm themselves enough to sign off on the American families who have already been vetted.

The ensuing week becomes an exercise in endurance. The chat room supported by our adoption agency blows up with panic, tirades, and pleas for a quick resolution to this crisis.

Having no way to contribute to the solution to this problem, I pack and unpack. I pace the floor. I practice mommy Romanian. I pray. Finally, the word comes: George's adoption decree has been signed, and we only suffered a one-week delay.

That's okay. We'll make it up to George, and ourselves. We will just keep celebrating from one side of the world to the other.

Getting to Romania turns out to be a pretty tricky business. The only reasonably priced flights to Bucharest are through Rome or Paris. I'm rooting for Rome, having never visited Italy. Joe is not willing to spend the extra five hundred bucks per ticket, so I let him have Paris. Who knows? Spending two nights in the most romantic city in the world might just be the miracle that causes our marriage to rise from the dead. Stranger things have happened.

Our first day in Paris begins with lunch. It is only 11:30 a.m. French time, but late enough to drink champagne and toast our incoming family member. Somewhere around the 13th arrondissement, we find a little bistro with fresh seafood on ice displayed outside. Feeling brave and a little giddy with jet lag, we make our way in. Neither one of us having any knowledge of the language, and our waiter not speaking English, we point at something random on the menu.

After drinking most of the bottle before us, we are eventually served small black-shelled mollusks, like mussels, but in miniature. They are so tiny, a special tool resembling a toothpick made of metal is provided to prick this bait out of its shell. Sufficiently sotted and still a little hungry from too much work and not enough food, I am ready to tour the shops and galleries of our host city. Perhaps a stop at a café for croissants and coffee.

My mood is spoiled when Joe, instead of getting carried away in the moment, insists on phoning home to speak to his folks. Even though we had cell phones, making international calls from them proved to be tricky. On the third try, Joe gave up. But he wouldn't be deterred.

I pout for a few minutes outside the telephone booth. He labors to place the overseas call, eager to connect with his source of support. A few moments before Joe emerges, I spot a cab. I'm deep in the fantasy of getting in and escaping unnoticed when he catches me. Before I can muster the courage to actually carry through with it, he says, "Great idea. I'm too tired to walk back. We should have a nap."

I can't even slap a smile on my face as we head back to our hotel, so I pretend to stare intently out the window, taking in the sights.

As the time gets closer to meet George, I am becoming increasingly anxious to get to Romania. The next two days pass in slow motion. The gargoyles at the top of Notre Dame Cathedral remind me that I should be soothing George's nightmares. Every meal eaten on rich cotton tablecloths stands in sharp contrast to the austerity of George's foster home. As I gaze at the *Mona Lisa*, her eyes seem to reflect wanting, and I project my wanting onto her.

Not even shopping soothes me. As Joe stands in the Longchamp store, credit card in hand, desperate to ease my angst, he says, "Buy any purse you want."

I cannot choose and emerge empty-handed.

On the third morning in Paris, we are finally on our way to the airport, to Bucharest, to claim our little Georgie. It is Christmas morning for me. I practically bounce on the seat of the taxi the whole ride there. The luggage is loaded on a hand cart; Joe pushes it, and we trundle into the airport. We look up at the Departures screen to locate our gate, but next to Bucharest, instead of a gate number, the word *Canceled* is flashing. There is screaming in my head, tears flowing so fast and hard I can't see, mouth agape in disbelief.

Leaving me with the luggage cart, Joe says, "Wait here—I'll go figure this out."

Little sobs escape from my chest as the minutes pass. Through a curtain of tears I continue staring at the word, now fuzzy through the wall of water over my eyes. My confidence in Joe figuring it out begins to wane.

Finally, I decide to figure it out myself. Pushing, then pulling on the luggage cart, it fails to budge, and I end up wheeling in circles, a slow-motion, weepy twirling mess.

When Joe finally returns, he says in his typical unruffled voice, "It's okay. We are going through Budapest. We will only be a couple of hours behind schedule." He pushes the magic little release button under the handle of the luggage cart. Just like that, he wheels us over to the check-in counter for our new flight.

There is free-flowing alcohol on this flight, and I, ever grateful to Dom Pérignon, the little monk who invented champagne, soothe my nerves with mimosas. Light on the orange juice, but a necessary nod to the fact that it's only seven a.m.

The airport in Bucharest is a jumble of confusion, what I imagine Bangalore would be with cooler weather. Passengers, weary and dirty from complicated treks across all parts of Europe, Arabic-sounding words yelled into cell phones, the most recognizable languages, Italian, Spanish, French, mixed with odd Russian-sounding endings of sentences. I spot the currency exchange booth and have Joe change two hundred American dollars into Romanian lei.

"Are you sure we need that much?" he asks, yet complies, returning with a wad of cash so thick that he can't even fold it, let alone fit it into the pocket of his jeans.

"Did you know there are over two thousand lei to the dollar?" he says.

As I joke that maybe we could buy the whole country with the bills in our hands, we split the wad of pink, green, and yellow bills, resembling Monopoly money more than American cash, between us, and hail a cab.

From the start of the ride, I am pestering Joe to get in touch with our contact here, a man called Matei. The irony is not lost on me that Matei is the Romanian form of Matthew, my first son's intended name. Joe insists that he cannot access the local phone system until we check in, so I content myself with staring out the window the entire thirty-minute ride to our hotel.

Once inside the InterContinental Bucharest, a hotel that would have been considered grand for the 1950s, we are met with acres of marble, gilt furnishings, and elaborately framed oil paintings. A cadre of burly men in leather jackets is seated in the lobby around the clock. They each have cell phones. At least a quarter of Romania's population lives on less than $5 a day. Yet, here we are, in a decidedly second world country, and every thug in the lobby has a cell phone pressed to his ear.

There is a note for us at the desk: "We heard your flight was canceled. George will be put on a train from Transylvania. It takes ten hours. He will arrive in the morning." Put my child through a ten-hour train ride? The train route from Transylvania to Bucharest is circuitous. The country is surrounded on three sides by the Carpathian Mountains, so travel by land is never a straight shot. The note ends, "If you have any questions, call Matei."

Which I have Joe do, while I panic and shake at the thought of this small, frightened boy traveling overnight with strangers. I don't know the details, nor do I wish to know them.

Joe somehow places the call, with a solid amount of assistance from the front desk clerk.

Matei's English is excellent, and he assures us that we won't have to put George on a train. Since we've arrived in town earlier than expected, he will meet us for dinner and explain the details.

Matei arrives clad in denim from head to toe. By the proud way he carries himself, I assume he believes he is well dressed, American style.

We are whisked into a taxi and taken to a restaurant called The Castle, and seated in a private room. We pass through the arches from one cavernous room to another, the white walls at least a foot thick, cement, textured, ancient. They emit a chill. The chairs are covered in rich brocade the color of merlot, the walls scattered with ancient-looking portraits. One features a man with stern face, dressed in burgundy velvet, captioned *Leopold, Prince of Hohenzollern*; another, a woman, captioned *Queen Muriel, Daughter of Czar Alexander II of Russia*.

It is late October, and the temperature outside is still in the 70s, yet the room is frigid. Matei assures us that this was a castle at one time and is now the finest restaurant in Bucharest.

Chateaubriand, a full roast, tender and cooked to a perfect medium rare and coated in sea salt, is served. Two bottles of Romanian cabernet emerge from the wine cellar. Caesar salad comes with Russian service, prepared table-side by our tuxedoed waiter. Appetizers, desserts, and cappuccino, and the bill is under one hundred dollars American.

Matei graciously allows us to pay the check and promises that he will be back at seven the next morning to accompany us to George's foster home.

CHAPTER 8
WELCOME TO TRANSYLVANIA

The flight from Bucharest to Cluj, the town in the district of Transylvania where we will claim George, takes only an hour, but it is a full sixty minutes of terror. The commuter aircraft has one seat on each side of a ten-row aisle. If I were not so determined and sure of my mission, I might have refused to board.

As I take my seat next to the hatch, I shoot Joe a terrified look, but he is already seated behind me, deep in conversation with Matei, across the aisle from him.

Later, in flight, I feel cold air flowing through the cracks of the hatchway. The little plane bumps and churns through the air. With each jolt, my grip on the arm of my seat tightens, as does the clench of my jaw. If I could have loosened my grip long enough to raise my arm, I would have summoned the flight attendant for drinks.

As I emerge from the plane, I make a mental note to put in my drink order right away for the return trip.

Our taxi speeds down dusty dirt roads. Signposts consist of hand-painted names on wood carved to point in the general direction of the *strata* in question. Class distinctions are dramatic here, evidenced by a Ferrari whizzing by, narrowly missing a cow that is wandering aimlessly through town.

Matei picks up his cell phone, alerting George's foster family that we are nearby.

The driver makes a sharp left and suddenly, we're here. He slams on the brakes, unprepared for the wall of people standing in the road to meet us. Grannies with babushkas on their heads, small children, dogs, all surround us. We are plunged into a B movie, a black-and-white horror flick.

I strain to find the little guy I am here to retrieve. From the crowd emerges a middle-aged woman in a pressed cotton shift and lace-up oxfords, holding George in her arms. They are both smiling.

I fly to her, and George reaches for me. *Mama*, he says, as I take him in my arms, tears flowing, but this time they are full of joy. Joe finds us, and George calls out *Tata*—Daddy.

We are led down a dirt path, to the same concrete house I recognized from the pictures, chickens pecking at our feet, goats and dogs in the yard. It is even more dismal up close, and as we approach the house, Joe whispers in my ear, "There is no glass in the windows."

Ornate blankets are laid across the threshold to welcome us, and we are seated at the kitchen table. It is sunny and warm outside, yet we are enveloped in a chill.

They insist on feeding the visitors, probably a month's worth of groceries and an entire slaughtered lamb. *Țuică* comes next, a homemade plum brandy, and sweets.

George giggles as I lift him onto my lap. The family smiles shyly, but does not speak to me, whispering only in Romanian, which I do not know well enough to decipher. There are other children living here, the niece and nephew of the foster family. They do not sit at the table with us, only hover in the background and watch.

As Matei chatters away easily to the family, I speak softly to George in the mommy small talk I had been practicing. I hold him close and plant little kisses on his cheek. *Vă este foame?* Are you hungry? *Iti place aceasta?* Do you like this? *Fii atent, e cald.* Be careful, it is hot. He does not react, but I am too anxious to get out of there to notice.

We have missed George's fourth birthday by a week and are served cake with a lit candle. George's face registers surprise. He does not seem to know what to do, so I help him blow out the candle. So far, George has eaten nothing, and does not even reach for the cake. I assume he has been fed before our arrival. There is nothing real about this experience; I push away the notion that even a child with a full tummy has room for cake.

We were instructed to bring gifts for the foster family, and we distribute them now. Joe presents Toma, George's foster father, with his topcoat, nearly new but no longer a good fit for Joe, which Toma doffs with a great show of gratitude and pride. Matei translates, "He will wear it to church every Sunday."

I bring Alina, George's foster mother, a bottle of Chanel No. 5, my favorite perfume. She looks confused when I hand it to her, like she doesn't know what to do with it. She smiles and sets it down.

When they insist on showing off their hometown, Toma is still wearing the coat, stopping anyone who passes, forcing them to admire it. We are ushered inside St. Michael's Church, a medieval structure, full of gothic pews and apses. I miss the descriptions of the artwork and English translation between Toma and Matei because I am chasing George. He is now our charge, but George does not seem to recognize that. He keeps running away from me, refusing to hold my hand. He seems to always be running in the opposite direction of where I want him to go.

Anxiety takes over. Afraid that I might not be allowed to leave town with my little treasure, I ask Matei, "Shouldn't we be going?" When he finally picks up his cell phone, it is only minutes before our taxi reappears.

Every inhabitant of this town seems to be circled around our car to get a better look at the foreigners and to bid George farewell. I want none of it, and focus on getting George and myself situated in the car, waiting for the crowd to disperse. I am afraid someone will try to stop us.

Plane travel in this part of the country is still a big deal, and children on planes are rare. George, now a celebrity, is taken to the cockpit to meet the pilot. From somewhere in the galley, cookies appear. In contrast to his behavior at the foster home, George now eats greedily, packing his mouth so full that I wonder how he can possibly chew. When the flight attendant speaks to him, probably to ask if he would like some more, she is already holding the treats aloft. He just reaches for them, not bothering to answer.

By now, I am too distracted by my new duties as George's mother to be frightened on this little plane, wiping his mouth from across the aisle and trying to keep up with the storm of crumbs flying unchecked. Apparently sated, he fails to stay in his seat, attempting to touch and climb on the few other passengers on the plane. Between the three of us, we wrangle George onto one or the other of our laps during the flight. He does not seem to understand the importance of staying seat-belted in this wiggly tin can.

Neither will he sit or wear a seat belt in the taxi. I am convinced that he did not ride in a car often enough to have learned to buckle in and stay seated. All the way to our hotel, I chat nervously to my little toddler, naming things as we pass. *Casa.* House. *Masina.* Car. *Camion.* Truck.

As we enter the lobby of our hotel, triumphant in our quest, the desk clerk comes around and claps Joe warmly on the back, shaking his hand. "Congratulations, Daddy," he says, and hands him a cigar.

This hotel is one of the most popular with American adoptive families. There is another couple seated in the lobby with a little girl, and they invite us over. They are together on a settee, a Rockwellian tableau, the dark-haired child, about seven years old, wearing a pink dress, legs crossed at the ankles. Her huge brown eyes are sullen, and she sits quietly while the new parents engage Joe in conversation.

While Joe joins them, I am left to chase George down the hallways and through doors marked *Nici o intrare*, No Entrance, as he explores the hotel. Or, rather, races through it. I chase him into the kitchen, all apologies. The wait staff stops in their preparations for dinner service long enough to search for a treat for this little one. As he zooms by, George is handed yet another cookie, and I stop trying to count the quantity of sweets he has already consumed.

Finally, back in the lobby, and hoping for some relief, I get George to pause long enough for me to grab Joe and get him to take a walk with us. We have not yet explored the streets of Bucharest, and I am hoping for help with the wrangling. "*Tineţi la mâna*—Hold my hand," I instruct George, but he races away from us, laughing. He has yet to speak another word to either of us, except the occasional *Nu*—No—but he seems happy.

He laughs and runs away. And then he runs away some more. He falls down. More laughter. Thirty minutes of chasing later, I am reaching the end of my rope. How could I possibly explain this comical scene, in my broken mommy Romanian, to the police? Two adults in hot pursuit of a toddler. This is obviously an attempted kidnapping. The prospect of being locked up in an Eastern European jail crosses my mind. I imagine a police officer asking George, "Mama?" and he, shaking his head and saying *Nu*.

Does he not like us? He doesn't know us; how could he like us? At this moment, I am not liking him very much, either. I push this thought away, still intent on having a celebration. It is so early in my relationship with this little one; it will take time for us to get to know each other.

Joe and I give up on the walk and resign ourselves to taking turns watching George in our hotel room. George bursts into the room ahead of us and immediately bumps into the luggage table, a pointy-edged makeshift piece of wood, roughhewn and sloppily attached to the wall. He falls down, laughs, and rights himself.

After assuring myself that George is uninjured, I decide to venture out. George had lost interest in the waddling duck on a string which follows him as he walks, our first gift to him. He left the foster home without a single toy.

"Be right back, with surprises for both of you," I say, determined to keep the atmosphere festive.

There is a grocery store down the street, a kind of general store with wine, toys, and food. The shelves are sparsely stocked, in sharp contrast to the twelve brands of peanut butter in every American grocery. Guards are posted at the meat coolers.

I spot a bottle of local champagne. The clerk looks up from the register when she sees that I am spending the equivalent of ten dollars American. With a sidelong glance, she says, "*Ah, șampanie.*" Champagne.

I answer, "Yes, it is a celebration," but she is still shooting me a snarky expression.

I also buy a stuffed bunny, a three-dollar purchase, not very soft but the only thing in this store resembling anything a child might want to play with. I have spent probably a week's wages for the woman before me. Apparently, sarcasm has no language barriers.

We pop the champagne while calling home for Joey and George to "meet." My little Joey carries the conversation with a couple of the phrases we have been practicing, punctuated with *Te pup*, literally "Kiss you," slang for "I love you." No response from George, but he seems amazed at the source of the sound, and spends the entire conversation staring into the handle of the phone.

The champagne is rancid.

Getting George ready for what Matei told us would be his first real bath, I peel layer after layer of grimy shirts from him. Under his pants I discover that he is wearing tights. Finally, the last layer comes off, revealing an angry red gash across George's rib cage. I realize this must be from when he hit the luggage table. There had been no tears when George fell, and now, seeing the injury, he laughs again. I chalk up the maniacal mirth to his being nervous around us, and attempt to dismiss it.

Not willing to risk another attempted flight on George's part, we order dinner in.

I get George settled into his pajamas with some difficulty. He struggles against putting his head into his pajama shirt. I finally understand that he is afraid of getting stuck. After several tries, the top of his pajamas is stretched out of all reasonable shape, but at least he's dressed for bed.

It isn't long before we are treated to the first of his coping mechanisms. George curls up, fetal position, and rocks himself, side to side, so violently that he shakes the bed. His arm covering his ear, a low moan comes from his throat, through the tongue sticking from his mouth. We attempt to comfort him, but he pushes us away.

The stuffed bunny flies across the room. Another reject.

The rocking continues for the next hour, and he finally dozes. But the lack of motion wakes him. And so, the pattern repeats, on and off, and on again, until morning.

CHAPTER 9
LOLLIPOPS AT THIRTY THOUSAND FEET

The next two days pass in a haze of sleep deprivation and rushing to appointments. First the medical appointment, where a female doctor clears him to leave the country. "*Nu verbest?*" she asks. "He doesn't speak?"

At the question, Matei glances at me. By the panicked look on my face, he registers that I understand just enough to know this part. He misses a beat, but answers "*Nu*," and continues speaking, everything else coming out of his mouth clearly beyond my level of understanding.

Beads of sweat start at the back of my neck, traveling down my spine, a cold chill, and a shiver. *She doesn't understand. He will catch up in no time. Dear God, what if she doesn't sign the paperwork?* There are several exchanges between the two of them, none of which I can decipher through the pounding in my head and my limited knowledge of the language. After I suffer five or six heart attacks, Dr. Marescue signs the physical exam report declaring George fit to leave the country.

Then on to the American Embassy, where George gets his picture taken and receives his exit visa. Matei makes his way to the front of the line, where women in babushkas pace, all seemingly in identical black lace-up walking shoes, their husbands smoking skinny cigars and showing off their white dress socks.

Joe has made sure to hand off the cash to Matei, as we were instructed. Two hundred and fifty dollars American, in denominations of tens and twenties, old bills, not newly minted. I find myself feeling sorry for these people who seem so used to waiting that when they are turned away for reasons spoken outside of my understanding, they are not surprised. They simply shrug and turn around, resigned to the fact they will now have to search for some derelict document or piece of identification. Or maybe they don't know the secret about the American cash. If they do, they don't have the grease to make these wheels turn.

We are ushered in and out like film stars. No waiting, prompt service. Papers are shoved before us and, at my insistence, we sign without reading the fine print. "We will read them on the plane," I say, and press the pen into Joe's hand.

We are stuffed into a taxi and on our way to the airport, Matei holding court from the front seat. He chats about the weather, and the fact that he will now go work out at the gym. He chatters away on his cell phone to someone, clearly a love interest, because he ends the conversation with *Te pup*. He is still unaccustomed to the fact that I understand some phrases. When I say, "Ah, your girlfriend," his face flushes slightly.

As we approach the terminal, it occurs to me that we have not been provided George's full set of health records, from birth through the present. The only reason I know that we are entitled to them is because I have studied the adoption packet, cover to cover. I know that Matei is charged with providing them to us, along with a journal his caregivers were required to keep.

"What about the records?" I ask, and although Matei's face registers surprise, he hands me a manila envelope, at least two inches thick, sealed. George's entire life story. In my hands.

"Do not open it until you get on the plane," he instructs.

Before I can question him further, we are deposited on the curb, and he is off.

Joe checks in the bags while I wrangle George, who is enjoying a new venue for his game. He runs away, laughing, and I, terrified and desperate, chase him.

When Joe catches up to us, he carries George through the jetway, but our little guy now refuses to be seated. Once we wrestle him into his seat, he will not put on his seat belt.

George has made a game of wandering off at every opportunity. He is intent on approaching and touching as many passengers as he can before we catch up to him and corral him back into our seats.

The flight attendants ignore us. The other passengers give us dirty looks, but one kindly older woman hands me an orange, which George attempts to eat by biting through the rind. I pull ammunition from my bag: lollipops, apples, crackers, and toys, anything that will mollify George long enough for us to take off. I may as well have left the picture books in our hotel room. He is not interested.

One of the lollipops, already out of its wrapper and sticky from being licked, flies forward three rows. I sink into my seat, lest the recipient of this little gift attempt to locate its source. Do I really think there might be one person left on this plane unaware of our little tempest?

As George finally resorts to the rocking which allows him to stay in one place, tears are rolling down my cheeks.

Joe looks over and says, "What's wrong?"

"I don't know," I answer, but the tears won't stop.

CHAPTER 10
LOVING GEORGE

It is breakfast time, and Joey and I are chattering away at George. We are talking *at* George because after two weeks at home, he has yet to respond to a single question, or utter a single word other than *Nu*, and the "Mommy" and "Daddy" we heard only once, in his native language.

Haila masa. Come to the table. George looks at Joey when he says this, but continues to punch buttons on the remote control, intent on finding the most violent television shows and recording random programs.

"George," I say, "if you want to eat, you need to sit at the table." *Stai la masă*.

He has been grabbing and running since we got him home. When I chase him and bring him back to the table, he grabs at whatever is portable and runs back to the family room. I chase him again and again, only to have him repeat the behavior.

He finally gets the message that food is to be consumed at the table. George's solution is to shovel food into his mouth as though it could be taken away from him at any moment. Then, he runs off, still chewing, cheeks bulging like a chipmunk storing up for lean times.

Doriţi suc? Would you like juice? Even though I show him the container, he fails to react.

Spalati pe dinti. Brush your teeth.

Te pup. Kiss you.

None of it evokes a response, yet flushing the toilet and switching the lights on and off seem to provide hours of entertainment.

I console myself with the memory of George's foster home. The windows had no glass; the toilet did not flush, nor did the light switches operate. It finally hits me that the children were not allowed to sit at the table. That's why he wouldn't eat anything in the foster home, even though the celebration was in his honor.

So, I sigh, and let him play with the toilet. I put up with the endless light then dark, then light again of the kitchen, as I attempt to make dinner.

I am convinced that George does not like me. How could he? He barely knows me. Because if that is not the explanation for George's strange behavior, and the utterance of one of the only words he seems to know, in any language, "no," I may have to face the possibility that something may be horribly wrong.

"I've got it." Elbowing Joe in the middle of the night, I bolt straight up in bed. "That's it. He speaks Hungarian. I don't know any Hungarian."

I remember having read in the background materials from our adoption agency that half of Romania speaks Romanian, but the other half speaks Hungarian, two languages with nothing in common. The words I learned sound Italian, with Russian endings. But there was that little detail about Transylvania once being claimed by Hungary.

Joe rolls toward me, eyes still closed, eyebrows raised. He is pretending to listen. With the same reaction he would have if I told him I forgot to pick up milk, he says, "Well, there's nothing we can do about that now."

He rolls over. The immediate soft snuffle of his snoring illustrates the depth of his concern with my latest problem.

The next morning, I'm on the computer, looking up Hungarian translation sites. I look at George, mouthing the newest, strangest words in my world: *Szeretlek*, George. I love you George.

Nothing.

Szeretne gyümölcslevet? Would you like juice?

Still nothing. Maybe I'm saying it wrong.

I had been prepared for something called reactive attachment disorder and try not to force affection on George too soon. The packet from our adoption agency had warned us that children who have been institutionalized often have trouble forming emotional attachments with their adoptive families. The longer a child remains in an institutional setting, the longer it takes for them to learn to react to family members with affection. George was alive, alone, and without us for the first four years of his life. So, when George pushes me away when I attempt to kiss him good night, or hug him in the morning, I am not shocked. And I don't push it.

And then there are his odd sleeping habits.

George's room is a wonderland of stuffed animals, books, and toys. His dresser drawers are full of clothing, his closet full of jackets and shoes. We had decorated his room in a sports theme, with football paraphernalia and artwork. The clock on his wall is painted to look like a baseball. We thought it was perfect for our little boy.

When George isn't rocking and humming himself to sleep, he stays up all night rearranging things. In the morning, his underwear is in the closet, his shoes in the drawers. We chalk it up to the sparse lifestyle of the orphanage, the lack of basic comforts in the foster home, no exposure to American culture. He will learn.

One morning as I come out of the shower, I find George in my room. Joe had gone to the office, leaving the belt he decided not to wear that day on the bed. When I emerge from the bathroom, there's George sitting on my bed with his stuffed Pooh bear, Joe's belt in his hand, beating the bear.

"Oh my God!" I shout.

I take away the belt before I can stop myself. He has no words, and this is the way he can tell us what happened to him before we got him.

The moment passes, and as much as I try to make eye contact with him, George resists. He abandons the bear and runs off. I feel like I've blown my only chance at getting a piece of the truth of his little life before us. It explains the scars that run up and down his spine.

I vow to handle it differently next time, to observe from afar and approach George gently, but I never get the chance. I had closed that door. George never repeats the behavior.

I am paying our handyman, ironically dubbed "John the Romanian," to translate the journal that came with George. I learn that George's birth mother was only fourteen years old at the time of his birth. The father was listed as "unknown." There are no details about why he had been given up for adoption.

By the time we got him, George was a beautiful little boy. Since his mother was so young and George probably looked like her, I assumed that she had been raped or was too young to support herself and had no choice but to give up her baby. I swear to myself that when George is old enough to understand the idea of adoption, I would find her and take George back to Romania to meet his birth mother.

According to the journal, after a year in the orphanage, George was transferred to his first foster home. He was encouraged to call his foster parents Mommy and Daddy, and his fellow foster children brother and sister. The foster father was killed in a truck accident six months after George's arrival, and his "brother" was adopted out to Spain.

George was then transferred to his next foster home. His behaviors were noted as odd. He would not stay in his bed; he would wander all night, and crawl into small spaces to sleep, rocking to soothe his demons.

When this family could no longer cope with George's nighttime somnambulation, he was transferred again, to the third and final foster home from which we claimed him. So much loss for such a little boy, and I cry after every translation session. John the Romanian would read, then pause, then shake his head. He would only sit with me for twenty minutes at a time, as though it was too much to tell. By the way he pauses, I can tell that he is weighing whether to hurt me with the words or make up something benign. I beg him to tell me, and he has no choice but to comply. His voice cracks as he tells me, in his halted English, what I need to know but do not want to hear.

There are nights when George will not stay in his bed, no matter the hour, so Joe and I take turns sitting at his bedside, enduring the rocking from side to side, hands covering his ears, until he sleeps.

He rocks, trying to block out the world, the now-familiar humming his own form of music. When he is asleep, we sneak out of his room, down the hall to our own bed. But it does not last. Ten minutes, fifteen at the most, and then George is crawling into bed with us.

"Let him stay," says Joe, and I try to comply, until the rocking commences in earnest. All elbows and knees, three to a queen-size bed. Finally, I can take him knocking into me no longer, and I take myself to George's room, letting Joe and George figure it out. But that will not satisfy George. He follows me, and there we are, the two of us together in his twin bed, George rocking and bruising me.

I try the couch. He follows.

I go to the spare room. He follows.

George is driving me to the edge of my sanity, and I am driving back.

One a.m. "George, get in your bed."

Two a.m. "George, leave me alone."

Three a.m. "For God's sake, George, stop rocking."

Thus, it goes, night after night, for weeks.

Until one morning.

I awaken, startled that I have been asleep for more than a couple of hours uninterrupted. Tiptoeing in my slippers down the hall, I peek around the doorway at George's bed. It is empty, and his comforter is gone. Knowing his affinity for small places, I open his closet. He is not there, either. Conducting a full search finally leads me to the hallway bathroom. There he is, sound asleep, curled up in a ball, camped out with his pillow and comforter, his head resting under the toilet.

You would think any parent in my sleep-deprived state would just let George sleep under the toilet. But that would mean acknowledging that something was amiss, and I am not prepared to do that. Having George sleep in his own bed becomes my mission, fitting him into the picture of what I want our family to be. All the while, that nagging little voice keeps up in my head. *Maybe sleeping is not his only problem.*

Like his continuing failure to speak. George had started school. He simply did not understand me or his teachers in either language. So, in agreement with the board of education, I enroll George in the English as a Second Language class.

The first day of school for George comes a few weeks after our homecoming. Supposedly settled in, he's ready to take on pre-kindergarten.

Until this day, I have allowed George to wander the house freely, pushing buttons, watching endless hours of television, switching lights on and off, flushing the toilet over and over, staying in his pajamas. He is getting used to his new surroundings, I reason. The easiest thing for me to do is allow him to explore his new home, where he is not interested in running away.

So, on this crisp morning right before Thanksgiving, my little toddler seems startled to be wrestled into blue jeans and a sweater. He rubs at my legs, and I realize he wants the tights he had been wearing when we first met.

"No, Georgie, honey; tights are for girls. You're a boy."

Hazel eyes stare at me, begging for the layer of comfort and security he knows. His little hands attempt to pull off the trousers, still rubbing my shin, as if that would make his beloved tights appear.

After much argument, mine verbal and George's in pantomime, he is finally washed, dressed, and manipulated into his car seat. Grateful for the car-seat latch that he has not yet learned to work, I maneuver the car, through George's head banging and screaming "No," the half-mile to school. All the while, I am talking, knowing George probably doesn't understand me. But I don't know what else to do.

"We are going to see your new school, George. It is going to be fun. You are going to make new friends. Your teacher's name is Miss Kelly."

When we pull into the parking lot, the struggle ends as abruptly as it began. A lightbulb has lit in George's head. A new place to explore.

I walk-chase him into the building and steer him into the school office. While I am speaking to the secretary, George slips by both of us. Before one of us can reach him, he has erased the computer screen. It is a tangle of embarrassment and "I'm sorries."

Miss Kelly arrives in the midst of the melee. "C'mon, George, let's go see your new classroom." She takes his hand.

Just like that, he is off to a new world, one apart from me.

The days run together as I wait for George to learn English. But he does not. He does not follow directions, and his teachers think he doesn't understand what they want him to do. His behaviors are getting stranger than they were when we first brought him home. The frustration of all the structure must be getting to him, because when he gets home after school, he acts out. Besides the normal constant toilet flushing and the light switches and the remote control, he refuses to comply with any simple request.

One day, when I lead him to the bathroom to teach him to wash up for dinner, he fights me.

The first time George hits me, it shocks us both. As I put his hands under the warm water and reach for the soap, he pushes me away with the strength of a fully grown adult. I stumble back but regain my balance and try to keep my tone even. I'm still trying to establish a mother–son relationship with George, even if he isn't ready.

So, I continue with the hand washing as best I can, try to forget the encounter, and set down his lunch.

It's funny; it seems there's nothing this child won't eat, and he always appears to be hungry. I try to slow him down, but whatever I set before him—today, peanut butter and jelly—he tries to shove it all in his mouth at once and then run away from the table, his cheeks so full of food I don't know how he gets it down.

"Slow down, George. Chew."

He doesn't seem to hear me, as he practically chokes himself with the stickiness of the peanut butter. Day after day, I've been letting the dog lap up George's spilled milk. None of it seems to get in George's mouth, and he ends up wearing more than he drinks. So now George has a sippy cup. He washes the food down as quickly as the slit in the lid will allow, and takes off for the family room, hands sticky with jelly, me in pursuit with a washcloth just in the nick of time before he can get to the remote control.

I let him play with the remote while I clean up the best I can.

The adoption agency had warned us to be ready for food hoarding. In the orphanages, the children didn't know when they would see their next meal. They shoved as much in their mouths as they could fit, as quickly as they could. Up until now, I hadn't let myself think about the possibility that this had happened to George. After all, he hadn't touched anything at the table when we were at his foster home.

I try to slow him down and make sure he can see there's plenty of food readily available whenever he wants, but he's so focused on devouring everything that is placed before him, it doesn't matter.

Carmela, the salon owner who styles my hair, is also Muriel's dear friend and neighbor. Throughout the adoption process, Muriel and Carmela, seasoned grandmothers, were cooing over our incoming family member, George. They were clucking about how lucky they were to have so many beautiful babies between them, and what a lovely time this was to be in our lives. I don't think Carmela was prepared for the child she met.

Carmela keeps a plate of doughnuts and a pot of coffee for her customers on a low table near the back of her salon. One afternoon, Joe comes to pick me up from my haircut with George in tow. As Joe tries to introduce him around, George makes a beeline for the doughnuts. I lunge for him, but George is fast. Before I can reach him, George has shoved the entire powdered mess in his mouth.

I throw over my shoulder, as casually as I can manage, "Oh, that's just George's orphanage behavior. He doesn't know when he'll see food again. He'll get over it."

I don't know whether it was the shock of the typhoon that was supposed to be our son swooping in and inhaling everything edible in his path, or the casual way I reacted. What was intended as a joyful moment of introducing George into the community turned into a cyclone.

This is not what Carmela was expecting as her friend's new grandchild. Disappointment was written on her face. As her jaw drops, Carmela's eyes get wide and watery, and they dart between George and me.

We leave the salon in the same cloud of smoke in which George had arrived.

Once in the car, Joe says, "You made her cry. Why did you do that?"

It occurs to me at this moment that I am starting to accept George's behavior as normal. But I push it away as a temporary situation and press on.

Nothing is making any sense, and it doesn't even seem weird to me that I have George convinced that if he wants to be in a store, he has to sit in the grocery cart or in his stroller. Although he's four years old, he's the size of a two-year-old. George is comfortable in the stroller, and since he doesn't know any better, I use it to my advantage. It seems the only logical solution if I want to take him out with me without fear of him wandering off. Whenever he tries to climb out, I shake my finger and say the one word he seems to understand: "No."

"No, George, little boys are not allowed to walk in stores. We'll have to leave if you get out of your stroller." Between my pantomime, my tone of voice, and the words he may be starting to pick up, he seems to believe me.

And that is how I get the grocery shopping and the errands done for the next several weeks. When I stand in line to pay for groceries, there are always extra weird foods in my cart that I would never buy, and I can usually sneak them back, at least to the endcap of the checkout aisle, without George noticing. He is too engrossed in the candy the store puts there to drive kids and their mothers crazy. If I hadn't seen the inside of a grocery in Bucharest, I would have thought his behavior odd. The scarcity of choices there stands in sharp contrast to the gloriousness that is ShopRite. It makes sense that George is overwhelmed by it all.

So here I am, with George in the grocery cart, trying to get our food shopping done. He's pulling everything that's not nailed down (which is just about everything in ShopRite) into the cart, and I'm prattling on about what to look for in the Rice-A-Roni aisle, trying to distract him while I sneak his choices back onto the shelves. The boxes and cans I put back are nowhere near where they belong. We don't eat Ragu (God forbid my mother see that—prepackaged Italian food was never allowed past our threshold), so it ends up next to the canned green beans. Package of pork rinds? In the frozen food aisle, on top of the Ben & Jerry's Cherry Garcia. (That's what I call job security for the store clerks who work here. You're welcome.)

My system is working well until the day I decide to make hot dogs and baked beans for dinner. I am prattling on about the ingredients we need, as much trying to teach George English as keeping him from throwing everything in his reach into the cart. Between telling him what to look for and redirecting his hands as he reaches for everything on the shelves, it takes a lot of energy just to get through the store. But it's better than chasing George around the house trying to get him to sit still to read a picture book or attempt a simple puzzle.

As we turn toward the canned goods aisle, there are two little boys, just about his size, running up and down the aisle, engaged in a game of tag while their mother is picking out sauerkraut. I turn the cart as quickly as I can, but not in time to hide the scene from George's sight. His first instinct is to stand up in the grocery cart and try to jump out. I catch him midair and wrangle him to the checkout line.

We get through the checkout, where George is now fascinated by Baby Ruths, trying to bite one through the wrapper. Okay, that one I buy, but I sneak the Milky Ways, Hershey Bars, and Bubble Yum back on the shelf while he's trying to swallow the candy whole.

I get George into the car, letting him struggle with trying to separate the candy from the half-eaten wrapper, so that I can buckle him in. He tries to clean his hands on my shirt, but I'm ready with wipes. Crisis averted.

Dammit, I forgot the stamps. The electric bill is due in three days, and PSE&G, our electric company, doesn't mess around. So, I pull around the shopping center and park in the only available space, directly across from Starbucks, but right next to UPS. I can get stamps there.

Walk-chasing George, he stops everyone to shake hands, and today is no different. A large black woman is in his path. He wraps his arms around her.

Before I can corral him, the startled woman recoils. When she realizes who has assaulted her, she smiles.

George has never met a stranger.

"It's okay, sweetie. Are you being a good boy for your mommy?"

I pull George away. The thought crosses my mind that I am getting used to being red-faced and apologetic. I push it away. Another crisis averted.

You know what really pisses me off?

When you walk by Starbucks and there's a guy lounging at an outdoor table, reading the *New York Times* while sipping a mocha-choco-latta decaf latte. Today I see this guy, forty-something, wedding-banded, pin-striped, hair slicked back. He's seated at one of the outdoor tables at the Starbucks, the store before mine, sipping his yuppie Gen X concoction and reading the paper, not a care in the world.

That's what pisses me off.

Where do these people come off relaxing while I'm just happy to get a brush through my hair sometime before noon?

Getting to the car is a trick because now George is out of control. He won't hold my hand, and he won't walk beside me. Now that he's had a taste of freedom and a little chocolate, George has decided that he won't sit in his car seat. And he's stiffened his entire body – his back is arched, his arms flailing. When I finally secure my child, I'm drenched in sweat. The flailing continues the entire ride. His little fists are clenched, and I'm bobbing and weaving my head to avoid being punched, but I can't escape the constant kicking of the back of my seat.

How we get home without crashing is still a mystery to me. I had unwittingly unleashed something in him, and although I don't know it yet, this is the beginning of a firestorm.

A few days later, I am standing at the kitchen sink, cleaning up from breakfast.

Last night's dinner is replaying in my head. It was like every meal since George had come to live here.

"George, if you want to eat, use your spoon. Sit down. No food in the family room."

Peas go flying, followed by utensils.

I am contemplating the tomato sauce on the chandelier, peanut butter on the ceiling. No use removing them. They will only be replaced by the beef stew I am planning on serving tonight. As I surrender to the idea of the permanent mess, it occurs to me that perhaps having food everywhere is not the only mess here.

The phone rings.

"Mrs. Thomas, we would like you to come to school to meet with the Child Study Team. George does not seem to be picking up English, and we feel he may need to be in the special education classroom."

Thus begins a series of meetings with this team, where George undergoes behavioral and psychological evaluations, IQ tests, and speech and language tests. Once the school district is convinced of George's inability to pick up language—English, Romanian, whatever—he is assigned to the special needs classroom.

Catching up takes time, after all.

CHAPTER 11
THIS IS NOT HOW TO DO SECOND GRADE

Although George has started school, he is only out of the house a few hours a day and is home by the time Joey returns from school. The three of us are sitting, if you can call it that, at the kitchen table, beginning an impossible second hour of second-grade homework. The endless delays are caused by George's constant reaching for his brother's schoolbooks, accompanied by "I want me"—in this case, George-speak for "Give me that," the endless mantra that is now the soundtrack of our days.

Not that he doesn't have his own pencils and paper. Every day, I sit George on the other side of the table and carefully write out the letters of his name, the letters he is supposed to be practicing. I start him out hand over hand, and coach him to continue. "See, George: G-E-O . . . good job. Keep going." Then, I race around to the other side of the table.

Joey is exhausted by the strain of attempting homework he doesn't want to do, the endless "I want me" interruptions, George's constant reaching for his pencil. He flops over in his chair, refusing to scribe the one simple sentence that will end this part of our agony for today. Joey isn't interested in school, and even less interested in homework. What's meant to be twenty minutes' worth of handwriting practice or simple mathematics turns into a two-hour affair, usually ending with my hand over his, guiding him, just to get it over with.

Joey is antsy in the classroom. One day, Mrs. Robinson calls me. Her chief complaints are that Joey's handwriting is messy, and he is falling out of his seat on a regular basis.

"I have checked his chair. I have changed his chair. Joey likes to kneel on his chair with his behind in the air. And then he falls out of it. He's disruptive, Mrs. Thomas."

It's not so much a complaint as an observation.

"If he weren't so intelligent, I would say he had a problem. Don't worry. He'll outgrow it. Someday he will have his own secretary. I just thought you should know. Actually, he's a delight. And the sight of him wiggling his behind in the air whenever he's bored, which is often, makes me smile."

How could I not know? He does the same thing at the kitchen table.

A few weeks later, we throw a Halloween party. Joey's friends are all in the basement, gorging on chocolate and soda, dancing and pretend-screaming at the gory decor. I hate Halloween, right down to the inflatable hearse Joe loves to put in the front yard. In spite of my attitude, we're really good at throwing Halloween parties.

For this one, my husband has created a full-sized effigy of himself. He's blown up a balloon and pasted a copy of his face onto it, and then stuffed a pair of his old jeans and sweatshirt to look like there was a body in them. To create the bed of nails on which his likeness lay, Joe covered ice-cream cones in foil and pasted them, pointed side up, on the door which doubled as a base for the electric trains he would run on them for Christmas. It's a pretty convincing resemblance—so much so that, even though my mother-in-law Muriel and I had a contentious relationship, I thought it cruel when he showed it off to his mother.

We've covered all the mirrors with sheets, let the silver tarnish, and placed stems of dead roses in vases. They include the pretzels I had formed to look like witches' fingers, the moles made from large chunks of sea salt, and fingernails from almonds covered in red food dye. The buckets of worms are made from Jell-O, gummy candy, and crushed Oreos.

George is stuffing himself but he's not bothering anyone, so we let him be. He's been indulging in all the sweets he can fit into his mouth at once, washing them down with bloody red punch from the witch's cauldron which is sitting on dry ice so it looks like it's resting on a smoky fire. I figure I'll deal with the consequences later, a small price to pay for the rare carefree look on Joey's face, surrounded by his classmates. King for a day.

But the storm doesn't come. When the kids finally clear out of the house, I find George curled up in his bed, sleeping soundly. I give up the tooth-brushing struggle in favor of peace. He will end up staying there until morning.

Before I leave his room, I stand at the foot of George's bed. I fight the urge to wrap him in my arms, rock him from side to side, and sing him a lullaby. Sleep is like gold around here, so I do it in my head instead. I imagine myself comforting my beautiful little boy, petting his curly brown hair, and telling him he is safe—that everything is going to be okay.

I believe that if he could only feel how much we love him, it would all be okay.

When his teacher calls the next day, I assume it's for the usual complaint: "Come and pick up George; he's disrupted the classroom, again." Instead, she says, "Mrs. Thomas, what have you done differently? George seems calmer."

We talk about the candy fest the night before and discuss the implications of something called paradoxical reaction syndrome. Mrs. O'Rourke tells me that some children have the opposite reaction you would expect from certain substances—usually medications in their system. Maybe the reason George didn't get hyped up on all the sugar and caffeine in his system was because he is one of those kids who has these types of reactions.

I tell her that her theory makes sense. I'd recently given George Benadryl for a rash, and instead of making him sleepy, as it does with most children, he got really wired.

She suggests that I discuss this possibility with his doctor. In the meantime, could I please allow George to have a little coffee with sugar or a Coca-Cola in the morning, before school?

I let the thought simmer. Maybe it would be good to try this—a little help until I can figure out the cure.

The coffee seemed to be working, at least for the first couple of hours of school. But the rest of the day was a loss. Mrs. O'Rourke couldn't control George and her classroom at the same time.

CHAPTER 12
GEORGE'S FIRST AMERICAN CHRISTMAS

It's a Saturday afternoon in December. We are due at the home of our friends, Faith and Eric, by 2:00 p.m. for their annual holiday open house. It's a party Joey looks forward to all year.

Faith and Eric have no human children of their own, just furry ones in the form of dachshunds, little hot dogs on four legs. Every Christmas, this generous couple spoils their friends' children with special toys and games. This party is designed for little ones, complete with an appearance by Santa Claus. And every summer, they hold a huge pool party in their backyard, with a barbecue, pool games, and water guns. A child's wonderland.

This will be the first time Faith and Eric meet George.

My husband always seems to find an excuse to go to the office on Saturday mornings, and today is no different. As I watch him swerving his BMW convertible over this morning's layer of flurries on the gravel of our driveway, I curse him for being quicker than me. If I'd just gotten myself ready sooner, I could have slipped out to do some ridiculously insignificant errand, leaving him to entertain the boys for the morning. He promises that he'll be home in plenty of time, but by 1:45 p.m., Joey is getting antsy, and the lights flicking on and off in the kitchen is beyond annoying.

I keep repeating "Party, party, party" to George like it means something to him, but having his brother in the car is enough of a distraction for him, and the possibility of a new place to explore keeps George in his seat long enough to get us to the next town in one piece.

Joe always says "I'm on my way" whether he's still sitting at his desk or in the car, on the road. Predictably, that's the answer I get when I call him. I tell him to just meet us at the party.

When we get to the door, Faith is there to greet us. She crouches down and reaches out to give George her first hug, but he's having none of it. Before I can get to him, George pushes past her.

As she tumbles to the floor, Faith is greeted by the sight of my little boy stuffing all the cookies he can fit into his little mouth, grabbed from the display on the dining room table. As he chews, crumbs come spewing out of his mouth, a sugary snowstorm, onto the rest of the platter.

As gracious as ever, Faith removes the platter. On her way to the kitchen, she hugs a visibly embarrassed Joey, saying, "It's okay. He'll learn."

Faith hands me an eggnog and puts her arms around me. I'm shaking and apologizing, even more upset that she is being so kind.

We are standing in a crowd of Faith's longtime friends and family members, all dressed in red and green, carols playing on the stereo, a Christmas movie on the TV in the living room. From the crowd emerges George. Without a word, he pulls down his pants and poops on the floor. No one speaks, but one by one, each of the guests turns and leaves the living room.

"I'll be in the car," Joey shoots at me, along with a glare that says "What have you done to me? I can't believe this." He stomps off into the snow.

I clean up George and the floor the best I can while issuing red-faced apologies over my shoulder as I shuffle George the hell out of there.

Joey and I have a heated exchange on the drive home.

"I hate him, Mom."

"I know you do, but he's your brother."

"He's not my brother," Joey says. "I didn't ask for him."

"I know, honey. It's going to be okay."

"How, Mom? *How* is it going to be okay?"

I don't answer him. I don't know whether it's going to be okay, and if so, how. But there's no time to think about that now. Our raised voices have upset the occupant in the back of the car, so we are treated to George kicking the back of our seats and rocking his head against the car seat all the way home.

If Joey had been at all bemused by the idea of having a little brother, his fantasy officially ends after the Christmas party. From this day forward, Joey is put out. He's embarrassed, inconvenienced, and unimpressed. This must be some kind of record. Under three months, start to finish and Joey is done with having a brother.

George wants to be included in his big brother's world, and Joey uses it to his advantage. A sneer in George's direction from Joey, a "You'd better behave if you want to go," from the boy he wants to be like, is enough to make George toe the line. Most of the time, but not enough for Joey.

CHAPTER 13

DOCTOR SHOPPING IN THE LAND OF DENIAL

As I work my way through the long line of experts, my world falls apart, piece by piece. Discounting the doctors is getting harder. We are exhausting the resources in our county, so I move on to Hunterdon County, the next one over from ours. The neurodevelopmental pediatrician there gives us global developmental delay, Attention Deficit Hyperactivity Disorder (ADHD, explosive behaviors secondary to oppositional defiance disorder and autism spectrum.

"Mrs. Thomas, developmental delay is a medical term, and *delay* really means *disability*. Not a temporary problem; a permanent one. We don't cure this. We deal with it."

"I don't want to medicate him," I counter. "There must be another way to treat this. Isn't there some kind of therapy?"

Dr. Gallagher meets my resistance with science.

"Look, Mrs. Thomas. Attention deficit disorder. Autism. They are diseases, just like diabetes. If I were telling you your child had diabetes, would you refuse to treat that, too?"

I let Dr. Gallagher write George a prescription for Adderall, a slow-release treatment designed to help George focus, but vow not to give it to him.

I don't want to give it to him, but George starts Adderall a few days later. When the medicine kicks in, it turns him into a zombie. And when it wears off, he's more violent than he is without it. I know this isn't right for George and stop giving it to him immediately, but I do start letting him drink a little skosh of coffee with lots of milk and sugar on school mornings.

Dismissing this doctor as a quack, I move on. I am now fully expert shopping. I summarily dismiss each one who does not agree with my determination to normalize George.

We see four psychiatrists in one week. Sitting on the side of the road in my car, yelling into the phone at my health insurance carrier, I demand to know why none of these doctors will speak to George. I insist that the way psychiatrists treat children must be seen as malpractice.

One after the other, the psychiatrists listen to my litany of complaints while I chase George around the room. Without engaging him or even making eye contact with George, they each write several prescriptions and tell us to come back in two weeks. Why had I put myself through the ordeal of bringing George with me? It was as though he was invisible to them.

By the time we leave the fifth therapist, she is in tears.

I am wrangling George, as usual. This is one of the rare occasions when my husband had an opening in his schedule and I was able to convince him to come with us. On this day, the planets had aligned, and Joe and I have George between us, walk-chasing him into the elevator to see yet one more psychiatrist. George still doesn't have names for us, although he had said *Mama* and *Tata* when we first met him in Romania. That was the last time he spoke them. Up until now, he has been pointing at things he wants or leading us over to them. The only word he has on repeat is "No."

When we get him into the elevator, the UPS man enters with us. He smiles at our son, and George reaches up for his hand and says "*Tata?*" "Daddy?"

I feel Joe's heart sink and mine sinks for him.

Joe has tears in his eyes as he whispers, "He doesn't even know I'm his dad."

Sucker-punched, I feel the air leave my body as another ray of light dawns. All the horrors of the orphanage, everything I had read about Romania cleaning up their act—could it be that none of it was true?

Nicolae Ceaușescu, who was a dictator but called himself the president of Romania until 1989, outlawed abortion and birth control in an effort to grow the country's population, and thus its workforce, after it was decimated in World War II. He confiscated many of the children and placed them in state-run orphanages. He believed that his regime could raise the children better than their parents could.

When the Berlin Wall fell, marking the end of communism in Eastern Europe, some despots didn't go willingly. Ceaușescu was one of them. During the Romanian Revolution, he and his wife were captured while attempting to flee the country. They were tried in a kangaroo court and executed by a firing squad.

When relief workers were allowed in the country, they found the orphanages were more like warehouses than safe havens. Some reports described them as death camps for children. The children were packed in, elbow to elbow, many completely naked, deprived of human contact, near starvation. Those atrocities caused the children to act out in ways that we were seeing in George. The indiscriminate friendliness, the unexplained rages with no apparent cause, the limited vocabulary, the endless rocking.

There was supposed to have been reform, and news stories promised that the orphanages had evolved. I understood that Romania was trying to join the European Union, and that this great disgrace had to be righted before they could be admitted. But had anything really changed?

Although I didn't want to believe that any of these horrors had happened to George, it was getting harder and harder to ignore what we were seeing.

I don't think Joe is aware of anything that happens during this appointment. I wouldn't blame him if he couldn't hear anything through the cracks in his heart.

It's the light switches that make it hardest to concentrate, so I try to let everything else go. If he would just stop flicking the lights, I could listen to Dr. Wilson while George played with her stethoscope or searched her pockets for her cell phone.

Her eyes are watery as she ushers us out of her office. "He's almost feral, isn't he?" she says quietly. A wild beast? Yes, I would say so.

I am overcome by George's behaviors—his failure to progress, my inability to fix it. I am wearing myself out trying to maintain a brave face and some semblance of normalcy for Joey, who is grossly inconvenienced by the brother he never asked for, and my husband is always in the office.

I am still convinced that we can love it out of him, but I don't have a clue how.

CHAPTER 14
MAYBE MY MOTHER WAS RIGHT

Once George starts in the special needs classroom, that nagging little feeling I've been having begins to grow.

It's June, seven months since we brought George home, and his behaviors aren't getting any better. He's not picking up English, he's not staying in his bed, he doesn't like us any better than he did the day we first met him.

Joe has taken to working more hours, conveniently coming home after he knows the kids will be in bed, working all weekend, and leaving me with my hands full . . . of George. My husband pretends not to hear me when I ask him, plead with him, to take George to the office with him, or to stay home so that I can get out of the house and take Joey to the movies, or out to lunch. He was having none of it. Fine.

Since my husband couldn't hear me ask for help, I couldn't hear him ask me to come to the office. My son Joey is alternately threatening to leave home or lock himself in his room forever, sometimes on the same day.

The light switches are still flicking on and off incessantly. The toilets never stop flushing. The remote control is always missing, usually turning up under George's bed, or in the dishwasher.

"I hate him. Make him go away. Mom, can't we send him back?" Joey's complaint was always the same.

"No, we can't send him back. He's your brother. You will learn to love him."

"He's not my brother. I didn't ask for him. He's weird."

I have no answer, so I give him none.

The day I reach the end of my rope is the day the boys won't stop biting each other.

George starts first. Joey bites him back.

"Stop it, stop it, stop it!" I'm screaming.

My seven-year-old looks up at me. "He bit me first!" Still making eye contact with me, Joey sinks his teeth into George's forearm.

George retaliates, going for the closest, largest target, Joey's thigh.

I'm desperate to make them stop.

I have a porcelain bowl on the kitchen table, my favorite. I had purchased it as a housewarming gift for our new neighbor. The hand-painted lemons match the sunny yellow of my kitchen. I liked it so much I decided not to part with it.

Before I can stop myself, I pick up my favorite bowl and hold it over my head. It flies out of my hands and smashes on the hardwood floor, shards of lemon-colored porcelain flying in every direction.

The boys freeze in place. I figure I've gotten their attention.

A mother's love can only take you so far.

I knew I needed a break; Joey needed a break; and I needed Joe and George to spend some time together.

My chance comes when my friend Sharon calls. She's in Charleston, throwing a fiftieth birthday party for our friend, Jan. "Why don't you come?" she says. "It'll be fun."

Joe isn't happy about the idea of being left with the boys for a long weekend. He's so unhappy that he refuses to give me the money to pay for a plane ticket.

I don't tell him that I'm planning on taking our older son with me, and I fix his wagon when Sharon sends me two tickets.

When I announce my plans, Joe gets so mad that he doesn't drive us to the airport or put any money in our checking account.

I get mad, too. On the plane, I start to figure out how Joey and I could stay in Charleston—what I could do for work, and which school I could enroll Joey in.

It's our third day in the Old City, and Sharon is still paying for everything. Every time I try to use my debit card, it's denied. But I'm not calling home. No way I'm going to give Joe the satisfaction of asking for money. I have no intention of going back.

We're standing on the Battery facing the Old Market when my cell phone rings. It's Joe.

"I put money in the account for you," he says. "I hope you two are having fun. When will you be home?"

With that one sweet act, I soften toward him.

"Tuesday," I answer.

When we return, there's been a miracle of sorts. My housework-allergic husband has made the beds. Things have been put away. He and George are on the sofa together.

It's a slow realization, but a realization, nonetheless.

My mother had a favorite expression for my sudden epiphanies regarding the everyday details of life. When I came to terms with something that she thought should have been obvious, she would say, "Ah, the light dawns."

She said it to me often when I was growing up.

As a child, I was gawky and awkward. Afraid of my own shadow, I was more comfortable in my room with a book than in crowds. Hour after hour, I would devour Nancy Drew books and imagine myself getting into dangerous situations and solving crimes. When my mother took me shopping for new clothes at Read's Department Store, I would try to replicate the tartan plaid skirts and headbands my heroine sported on the covers of my favorite books.

I was the youngest in my class; my dad had snuck me into first grade months before I turned six years old. I was always reading above my grade level because I was always reading. In the fourth grade, I chose to write a book report on a five-hundred-page book about Lizzie Borden, who took an ax and gave her mother forty whacks. Mrs. Palermo, my teacher, called me up to her desk. She quizzed me on small details until she was satisfied that I had read the book myself.

Immersing myself in the imaginary worlds presented before me by the mere flip of a page was a lot more interesting than the workings of the vacuum cleaner or the reasoning behind separating whites from colors. Why? All the clothes got clean anyway. The day I pulled my white panties out of the washer and they were magically pink, I realized why you have to separate the whites from the colors. With a smirk on her face, my mother said, "Ah, the light dawns."

She meant that I was book-smart but had no common sense.

Maybe she was right. Maybe she still is.

The light was dawning. Maybe we had more than a little problem on our hands.

CHAPTER 15
CHEMISTRY LESSONS

We are approaching our first full summer with George, and still no discernable progress. The line of experts is long and expensive. I'm still convinced that their job is to find a cure. My job is to force them to tell me what I want to hear—that George is simply delayed and would catch up.

I am learning to conference with doctors and chase George simultaneously, a skill I will need over the next several years. George explores each examining room. He ignores the toys placed on the floor for his benefit in favor of flipping light switches and running water in the sink. Between redirecting his hands and my new litany—"No, George, don't touch; play with the toys, George"—I attempt to digest what each doctor is trying to explain.

We start with the most obvious doctor, the pediatric neurologist from the local hospital. She is recommended by George's pediatrician. In an effort to gain some support, I start taking Muriel, my mother-in-law, with me. As temporary as I consider our problem to be, I need some help.

But this doctor is so unfamiliar with the situation that George had come from that her report is inconclusive. She has concerns around his expressive language and concludes there is evidence of minor motor delays. She says that a diagnosis would be difficult to make at this time, and then she sends us on our way.

Muriel uses these sessions to soothe her conscience for not babysitting George during the two hours of hell that comprise second-grade homework for Joey. She insists that there's nothing wrong with George; I just don't know how to talk to him. Maybe I am provoking him. Maybe the problem is with me.

I stop taking Muriel to doctors' appointments with me.

CHAPTER 16
THE WINTER OF MY DISCONTENT

A long string of appointments continue through the summer.

The latest report, from a speech pathologist, says "He will never speak the way we do."

I know how the babies used to be fed in Romanian orphanages before Romania joined the European Union, but all the articles I've read and news programs I've watched assure me that things have improved since then. A hole the size of a dime would be punched into the nipple of a baby bottle, and a sort of glug would be placed in the bottle. A fast way to feed many children in a short amount of time, with limited supplies and nutrition. For children to keep from choking, they had to plunge their tongues to the back of their throats so that the glug wouldn't suffocate them.

George has a lack of "phonemic awareness," the sense that tells you where your tongue is in your mouth, to make words that sound like words. Could it be that George was fed this way? Even if he were, I am convinced there has to be a cure. I push off the speech pathologist's report and chalk her up as being a cynic. If she weren't so negative, maybe she would give me the clues to solve this puzzle.

Still determined to find the fix, I am on to the next expert, a child development specialist who is also a neurologist, hoping against hope that he will refute the other doctors' reports. But his prognosis is worse than my wildest imaginings. "He will never fit in," the doctor says. "This child belongs in an institution."

The thought of this small boy in my idea of an institution—strapped to a bed in a long row of patients, medicated and crazed—is enough for me to label this doctor a cynic, as well. But this doctor gives George Clonidine, a blood pressure medication used off-label to treat sleep disorders. George is finally sleeping through the night. And that means that I am, too. Maybe I'll let George continue taking it until we find the cure.

I continue on my quest for the cure, but I am running out of child development specialists. The diagnoses now include mood disorder, bipolar disorder, autism, attention deficit hyperactivity disorder, and general developmental disorder. The doctor who gives me this list also gives George Risperdal, the drug that treats all of these disorders, along with the anxiety the disorders cause in its sufferers. For the bipolar disorder, George receives Depakote. After a few days, I'm finding large clumps of his hair on his pillowcase. We switch to something called Gabapentin immediately, but the damage is done. After a few weeks, a bald spot appears on the back of George's head. George went completely bald, right down to his eyelashes and eyebrows. It took years for the hair to grow back. When it did, it was magnificent... lush and curly. To this day, George has spurts of alopecia. I'm just grateful he can't see the back of his head.

This doctor also prescribes a variety of Attention Deficit Hyperactivity Disorder meds for George, one after the other, until we find one that has the fewest side effects. Dosages went up. Dosages went down. One drug gave him a beer belly, another took his appetite and made him too thin.

Since the Adderall made him more violent, we tried Ritalin. That's when George developed his swimmers' physique. I thought ADHD meds were supposed to settle children who were hyperactive. George seemed calmer, but he couldn't stop rotating his shoulders. He looked like he was performing the butterfly stroke. I got clocked in the jaw more than once. Since he couldn't control it, we never knew when George was going to take a swim, and if you happened to be walking by him at just the right moment, you were in danger of being elbowed in the face.

We finally settled, for the moment, on Dexadrine. If George was suffering from dry mouth or headaches, he was not showing it. Without the words to tell me, I only had to assume that he was okay.

By now, George is at least controllable in the classroom for short periods of time, even if he is not fully paying attention. I had been fighting the idea that medication might be the answer because I'm still not ready to concede defeat. I'm George's mother, and I should be able to solve any problem for my child. If I can't, that makes me a failure as a mother.

But the sleep is so precious. That kind of prize helps me deal with the guilt of giving in to the medications. Just for now. A temporary reprieve, but a reprieve nonetheless.

I didn't know that *just for now* would turn into years of searching, years of hoping—that Joey and George will start to get along, or that Joey will at least tolerate his little brother while I am figuring out how to make it all better. For everyone. I watch Joey go through the motions as he attends second, third, and fourth grades, the routine of going to school, coming home, hiding in his room, pretending he is an only child. I keep wishing I could give him something to hold onto.

I can feel my grip on normalcy slipping. So far, my hands have been clenched around the picture of the happy little family I hoped we would become. The earth under my feet is beginning to shatter, piece by heart-breaking piece. As I drift off into a wine-induced coma each night, sadness slips through the cracks. The fantasy I have set for myself isn't holding, and each night, as my head hits the pillow, tears sneak out of my eyes. They will no longer be willed away.

Each expert unwittingly confirms the other. I reject their pronouncements but not their prescriptions. And I get some help of my own. I allow my doctor to prescribe a little antidepressant, telling myself, not convincingly, that everything will be okay.

As I swallow a Lexapro, I tell myself that I'm taking it, just for now.

CHAPTER 17
ENTER "THE EMPEROR"

It's a rare Friday evening when Joe is home; we've had dinner together, or what we now call dinner, with George flinging food and Joey complaining about how inconvenienced he is by his entire life.

I'm upstairs, having Joe help me wrangle George into his pajamas, when the phone rings.

It's Muriel. "Quick, turn on *Dateline*."

The closest TV is in our bedroom, so we perch on the bench at the foot of the bed. We watch as Dr. Ronald Federici methodically reintegrates a sixteen-year-old Romanian boy into his adoptive family. A neuropsychologist and acknowledged US expert in the adoption maladies of Eastern European adoptees, Dr. Federici has been dubbed "The Emperor" for his matter-of-fact approach, the composed way in which he issues directives, and his reputation for calming the demons that follow Eastern European children into their new lives.

George sits between us, mesmerized, as though he recognizes someone on the screen.

The story follows a family who put their lives on hold and dedicated themselves to the behavior modification therapy that Dr. Federici prescribed. The family had struggled alone for ten years since adopting their son, Dane, from Romania. Now, with Federici's intervention, they are concentrating on streamlining their son's life, simplifying his surroundings and sensory input. The entire family is being trained in how to appropriately interact with their child, and Dane is also being taught appropriate behaviors.

Talk therapy is initiated. Dane gets angry, and as he rages, Dr. Federici teaches the family how to calm him.

The protective hold is the hardest thing to watch. As Dane struggles, one parent or the other places Dane on the floor, legs and arms secured, a move designed to protect him and anyone else who could be injured because of his rages. Hour after hour, this child in the body of a man twists, screams, and sobs, but eventually, he relents. He weeps, sighs, and rests.

After a full day of one such struggle, the family sits down to dinner together. It works.

Finding the cure for George's ills is now only a phone call away.

I can't ignore the irony that Muriel, the very woman who insisted that there is nothing wrong with George is the very same woman who discovered the cure.

CHAPTER 18
CHEMISTRY MEETS VODKA

An entire year of wandering about on my own, piecing the clues together to this unsolvable puzzle, but now I am carrying my family to the door-step of victory. I consider myself lucky to get us an appointment so quickly, with a doctor who is obviously in national demand, and excited to finally find the answer.

Three months after the *Dateline* piece airs, and several thousand dollars later, Joe and I are sitting in the office of "The Emperor." As usual, George is looking for something to explore.

"Bring him in unmedicated" was Federici's first directive. I wasn't sure what to expect from a drug-free George, but I wasn't expecting this. The entire ride from New Jersey to Virginia, I was in the backseat, struggling to keep an untreated George mollified so that Joe didn't crash the car. While George kicked me, punched me, and spit on me, I told myself that the longest six hours of my life would be worth it once we got the keys to unlock the cure to George's issues and started down our road toward a normal family life.

When I was able to wrangle him into his car seat and keep him there, George would bang his head against the headrest, all the while screaming "Help!"

I'm helping as fast as I can, George.

We are finally in the waiting room, suspiciously bare of the expected toys, magazines, and other distractions meant to keep waiting patients busy. But the walls are breathtaking. Filled with original oils in the style of the modern painter Itzchak Tarkay, with the wide swaths of rich color, paintings of women at tea, interacting with their surroundings.

Once inside Dr. Federici's office, we are greeted by two hand-painted urns, each the size of a toddler. He starts to explain that the collections we are seeing are from his frequent trips to Russia and Romania, artists he has discovered there.

But the pleasantries end abruptly when, without warning, George starts to twist, spit, and flail, attempting to find contact with any part of the good doctor which would take a punch or a bite. As Dr. Federici picks George up by grabbing hold of the back of his shirt, very much resembling the way you would hold a puppy, he orders, "Go and get his medication."

Joe is only too happy to excuse himself for the ride back to our hotel. While he's wrangling George, Dr. Federici asks, "Did you see the *Dateline* story?"

I answer, "Yes, that's how I found you."

"What did you think?"

"I thought it was scary. But we're ready."

He deflates my balloon, just a little, when he adds, "There are things they didn't tell you in that piece. The situation was much worse than what you saw on TV. And did you read my book?"

No, I hadn't.

With his free hand, the one that's not holding George like a puppy dog, Federici reaches behind his desk and produces a copy of *Help for the Hopeless Child.*

A promising title. I hold the front cover open so he can inscribe it.

George is now medicated. "The Emperor" is back in charge. He sends us away for the afternoon, and it is glorious… for Joe and me. Lunch in a French restaurant, with escargot, lots of garlic and wine. We are predicting success and enjoying every moment of our perceived triumph. Intoxicated shopping is always the most fun, and after this wine-sotted luncheon we got a new wallet for Joe, a book for our Joey, and a silk scarf for me. When we finally stroll back to the office at the appointed time to claim our little boy, we find that Federici didn't have quite as pleasant an afternoon as we.

We enter the office of "The Emperor," and are greeted by a visibly disturbed Dr. Federici. His hair is pointing in odd directions. The knot in his tie is strained, like one side had been yanked on. And he had what looked like bite marks on his shirt.

We are handed back our child and ushered out of the office. It's a two-day evaluation, and George is due back here tomorrow at 9 am. Promptly. I thought I heard "The Emperor" mumble something like "don't come back", but I told myself I heard him say "See you tomorrow, can't wait."

On the second day of George's evaluation, Joe and I arrive to see that the urns had been removed.

"What happened?" I ask.

"I'd like to keep them" was the doctor's answer.

Neither was he sporting a silk tie, the way he was dressed when he first greeted us. I assumed he wanted to keep that, too.

After an intense two-day evaluation during which George was either hugging, punching, or ignoring Federici, the doctor delivers the bad news. Not only could Dr. Federici not cure George, but our child's prognosis is even worse than Dane's. George's intelligence level isn't even high enough to respond to the treatment Federici had designed, and the length and level of neglect George had experienced in Romania was even more intense than Dane's. Dealing with the symptoms, not the disease, would be our fate.

Worse yet, after reading the full report on George, in its original Romanian, Dr. Federici says, "Your translation was wrong. They knew all of this."

There's more. He saves the worst for last.

"George suffers from fetal alcohol syndrome."

Fetal alcohol syndrome (FAS) is a disability which occurs in utero. When a pregnant woman drinks, even moderately, the intake of alcohol can cause cognitive damage, growth problems, low birth weight, developmental problems and behavior issues, namely enormously violent outbursts. FAS wasn't getting much attention in the United States by American doctors, at least the ones we were seeing. Looking back on our tour of medical experts on the East Coast, not one had yet suggested FAS. I don't think American doctors recognized it, so no one knew how to treat it. Or maybe Dr. Federici was so used to seeing it in Eastern European children, that he was hyperaware of the signs. The lack of funding in the US to bring awareness, prevention and treatment didn't help, either. In recent years, federal funding declined from $27 million to just over $12 million. In the United States, heavy drinking or drug abuse during pregnancy which causes damage to the fetus is looked down upon, and some states had outlawed it. Some had gone so far as to impose reporting requirements on medical professionals, whether or not there were repercussions to the fetus. But there is no national agenda, no unified policy. The federal Fetal Alcohol Respect Act is now seeking to raise funding, awareness and prevention for the estimated one in 7 pregnancies, by some estimates, affected by alcohol.

In Romania, however, there is very little, if any, prenatal care, and FAS is common, caused by high intake of alcohol while pregnant. There is widespread use of home-brewed plum brandy, on the order of moonshine. It is grain alcohol, beyond any alcohol content considered safe here. I think it's safe to assume that George's mother had consumed a fair quantity while she was carrying him. The violence that I was the primary victim of and witness to, was all the proof needed to confirm George's diagnosis.

Once Dr. Federici pointed out the facial characteristics of FAS... George's misshappen ears, eyes too wide set, the flat space between his nose and his top lip, I saw it, too. I couldn't wish away the knowledge, the sudden realization, the light dawning.

I'm spinning into a vortex, and struggling to get my eyes to focus, drowning in bad news, sinking into it and being swallowed by it.

"*Who* knew all of this?" My mouth forms the question, but it comes out more like a squeak than my voice.

"The orphanage knew. The foster homes knew. The adoption agency. I hate to tell you this, but passing off handicapped children as normal has a higher profit margin than the normal ones. The agencies get the children cheaper, and then they sell them to you."

Federici was past using politically correct terms like *disabled* or *special needs*. He was as angry giving me the information as I was sucker punched receiving it.

He continued. "Adoption agencies get away with it because they never touch your reports. They can claim ignorance that way. Did you get any medical reports from your adoption agency?"

I can only shake my head in the general direction of 'no', but I confirm his suspicions. Our reports all came directly from the foundation in Romania that handled getting George to us. Our adoption agency never saw them or touched them.

"Don't feel bad," Dr. Federici says. "You're not the only parents this happens to. They see a video; they fall in love. Logic goes out the window."

He was right. How did he know that the moment I saw George I lost all connection with reason?

The doctor's closing salvo? "You've got a life sentence on your hands."

The problem with a visceral reaction is that once the emotion fades, you're stuck with reality. He is right. We had fallen for George at first sight and had ignored all the signs, all the evidence that there could be something amiss. I had been blinded by love; I was blinded, and I tried to force Joe to be blinded, too.

The solutions Dr. Federici could offer us are few. We are stuck with coping mechanisms, no permanent solutions. He tells us to clear George's room of everything but the bare necessities, to avoid too much sensory stimulation. He reviews George's medication list and suggests some minor changes. He trains me in protective holds to minimize the damage to George and ourselves when George rages.

There would be no talk therapy. There would be no cure. There would be no sense of the normal family life I had dreamed about.

Just for tonight, we tell ourselves, we will sit in the hotel bar, George between us, happily downing all the Cokes he can fit into his little body, and we will drink vodka until we are numb.

This isn't how I anticipated the day going. I thought by now I would be planning a celebration for a month from now, having hope that George's fifth birthday would start to resemble a typical family life. Instead, our hopes dashed, Joe and I spend the evening of our tenth wedding anniversary, in total silence, drowning our biggest sorrow.

CHAPTER 19
THE REPORT'S IN THE DRAWER

A large manila envelope arrives in the mail. I know it's Dr. Federici's report. I let it sit on the desk in the kitchen for a week before I bring myself to open it. Inside is the death knell, the point of no return. I know what it says; Dr Federici told me. There's no point in reading it. I know that once I see the words, in black and white, there will be no more denial, no more hope for the family I so desperately want us to be.

When I finally gather the courage to break the seal, my hands are trembling.

Twenty-eight pages.

It starts with a list of the testing that George went through during those two days; and the tests that were attempted but couldn't be completed because of George's short attention span or limited IQ. Then, the background information that made us seem like a normal family looking for a second opinion about their child's lack of adaptability and odd behaviors.

I start to read but have to put it down before I get through the second page, mostly because I can't see through the tears that flow once I get to "George has many complicated medical and psychoeducational diagnoses." The rest of the page is now a blur. I know what's coming, and there is no willing it away.

It takes me a week to get through it all. The light dawning has never been as painful as it is this time, but I know the only chance I have to win my battle with the board of education—to get George into the special needs school I need him to attend—will be found in this report. So, I take it in bits, punctuated by crying fits. And force myself to read on.

"There is no cure, Mrs. Thomas. You have a life sentence on your hands," is on repeat in my pounding brain as I try to digest the medical terminology in front of me.

Now that the review of all the prior testing has been put in one place and digested in this one report—the evaluations from the neurodevelopmental specialists, the various school specialists, the three years of looking for the cure before we found "The Emperor"—I am starting to feel ridiculous. They say that hindsight is always 20/20. In reality, the pieces had been in front of me all along, like a puzzle I was too close to, to solve. Forest for the trees and all that. I should have known, but I didn't want to know.

At almost seven years old, George has the mental capacity of a twenty-one-month-old; he scored in the severely autistic range, and his IQ tested out at 53, considered clinically mentally defective. Compared to other children of his chronological age, George is in the bottom one percentile across the board. That means adaptive skills. The ability to control his reactions to his surroundings is missing in his brain. He cannot process waiting his turn or even what happens tomorrow. Everything is in the here and now. At least he's living in the present. Isn't that what we're all supposed to be doing?

His ability to learn is affected. Dr. Federici had told me that, as he grew, George's IQ would test even lower. Because George would not progress at the same rate as other children his age, and those are the children he would be tested against, he would continue to fall below the mean.

"George is grossly impaired in receptive and expressive language; personal, domestic, and community activities; in addition to interpersonal relationships and coping skills. George requires constant attention, supervision, and structure as he is just unable to self-regulate even with the assistance of medication and very strong educational and parental support."

There it is. The undeniable, permanent prison sentence that would define the rest of our lives.

I now have a new list to add to our growing list of diagnoses:

Dementia, probably due to fetal alcohol syndrome; post-traumatic stress disorder; below average intellectual function; neurodevelopmental disorder, also caused by fetal alcohol syndrome; along with all the unusual physical maladies that plague him. This includes alopecia (his hair falls out every once in a while); his hearing (even though his hearing tests as normal, he has had tubes placed in both ears, and is prone to frequent ear infections); and his vision (which is poor, even with glasses).

George is subject to strange illnesses, and I find myself calling our pediatrician almost weekly. George came home from school one day, scratching an angry red rash covering his chest and back. I plunged him into an oatmeal bath, attempting to soothe his itching and make him stop scratching. It looked like hives. I put up with George struggling against getting into a tub full of breakfast food but forced him to take the cure. It didn't work. When I described the breakout to Dr. Franklin, George's pediatrician, he said, "It's scarlet fever."

"Scarlet fever? Who gets scarlet fever anymore?"

George, apparently.

Scarlet fever is rare and is usually a side effect of strep throat and fever. George doesn't know how to complain or let me know when he's not feeling well. My only indication is his tendency to put his head down on the kitchen table when he's getting a cold or an ear infection. He had done none of that this particular time.

The hardest thing about loving George is being subjected to his outbursts. Remembering that when he's raging, he's gone, that he cannot form the intent to hurt us, is the only consolation. In criminal law class in law school, we studied the elements of a criminal act. One of the most important ones is intent. If you hurt someone on purpose, that's the worst and highest level of crime. If you hurt someone just knowing you are doing it, but didn't do it on purpose, that is the second worst. If you hurt someone recklessly, then you just did dangerous stuff without considering the consequences. And the least harmful level of intent is negligence. That means you were just careless, and someone got hurt because you just weren't paying attention.

The best defense is always an insanity defense, because it means that the defendant could not form the intent to hurt someone, or to appreciate the consequences of their actions. If the judge or jury buys it, the defendant usually gets sent to a mental health institution, not jail.

George had committed no crime. He couldn't have intent. That would imply he knew what he was doing. And he wasn't insane. Insanity implies something you can recover from.

I know now that I must be resigned to a life of mere survival. To suffering at the hand of our child, protecting ourselves from him the best we can, shielding Joey as much as I'm able. I don't know how to fix it because there is no fix. There is no way out.

CHAPTER 20
SOMETIMES, EXTINCTION IS A GOOD THING

When Dr. Federici trains me in protective holding, he teaches me about extinction behavior. He tells me that once George's rage gets to a certain point, George will give it one more shot. If I can get past that point without heightening the rage, George will realize he is not going to get the desired interaction from me and will naturally calm down.

It seems I need a little extinction behavior of my own. In an effort to continue the little facade that we're integrating George into our family, Joe and I are still inviting our friends in for dinner.

As Marci and Duncan, longtime clients in the law office, and now our friends, sit at our dinner table, George discovers a new way to communicate. Besides his stock "No," George has now learned "I want me," the only three-word sentence he would utter for the foreseeable future. It means everything. *I want some. It's my turn. I want to go, too. Give me that.*

But he also has other communication skills.

As George reaches for the roll on Duncan's plate, I say, "Georgie, no. You have your own. Here, eat this."

But I'm not quick enough. As I pull George's hand away, his head jerks forward. Before I can register the act, his face still calm, George has bitten Duncan's hand. Hard. He draws blood. My "NO, GEORGE. NOT NICE" proves just the encouragement George needs for his next phase of communication. I have unwittingly flipped on the violence button, the calling card which he would carry for the next nine years.

As Marci and Duncan look on, their mouths hanging open, the curtain drops. George's face twists into a knot. He is gone, replaced by the storm he is about to unleash.

He lashes out at the nearest target; I place myself in his way. While Joe continues to make small talk with our guests, pretending nothing unusual is happening, I have managed to wrestle George into the kitchen. His arms flail, clenched fists seeking contact. As I gather George into the protective hold that I have had too much practice at already, he lands a punch.

Following Dr. Federici's instructions, concentrating on keeping no expression on my face and as little intonation as possible in my voice, I cradle and comfort George, but I don't know how much he hears. I become aware of droplets of sweat dripping from my face; George is so involved in his meltdown, he doesn't notice that his shirt is wet from my exertions. "It's okay, George. Mommy loves you" is the anaphora that will eventually make the raging stop.

When he is finally spent and convinced of my lack of reaction, George relents. As his body relaxes and his crying subsides, I know it's safe to let him go. But the cradling and comforting that are supposed to happen next never take place. George is on his feet, "TV" on his lips as he makes for the remote.

Free rein over the remote is a small price to pay for another glass of wine with my friends. So, I give in and let him watch whatever he wants on TV.

By the time I pull myself together enough to return to the dining room, Marci and Duncan are gone.

CHAPTER 21
BETWEEN A ROCK AND A HARD PLACE

One by one, our available social outlets and opportunities for relief are beginning to crumble. Over the next several years, I would become a pariah to my friends.

Sharon and I met while we were both in college. I was majoring in political science and, during junior year, was given the opportunity to represent Fairfield University in a seminar held in Washington, DC. Sharon was there representing the College of Charleston. We bonded over breakfast.

"How are your grits?" I asked.

When she responded, "As bad as yours," we became fast friends and soon considered each other close confidantes. I had visited her in Charleston so many times that after graduation from college, I moved there to be close to my friend. Until I entered law school three years later, I considered Charleston my home, and planned to return there, law degree in hand.

Once I'd met and married Joe, I knew I would have to make New Jersey my home, at least for a while. Joe needed to be near his parents. Years later when Sharon married and moved to Florida with her new husband, we formed a plan for me to move my family to the Palm Beach area so that we could live near each other. Sharon and I had been inseparable for almost two decades.

There is an article in the *New York Times* about a ranch in Montana that is performing miracles with traumatized Eastern European adoptees, mostly Russian, but some from Romania. American parents, parents who are at the end of their ropes, driven to the edge of insanity by their children's odd, maladaptive, and sometimes dangerous behaviors, are sending their children to this ranch, where the children are subjected to regulation of their sensory input, placed on horseback for therapy, and given chores to perform. The goal is to reintegrate the children into the family unit. As a last resort, those who cannot be managed by their adoptive families are sometimes rehomed, adopted all over again by families familiar with post-institutionalized children and ready and equipped to deal with them.

Sharon sends me this article.

I'm sitting on the swings in the backyard with Joey on a day in early June. It's sunny but still cool enough to enjoy being outside. It's a rare day off with just Joey and me. Catholic schools recognize saints and give students days off to pray to that saint, presumably. We used it to do just this. George is in school, and I'm enjoying a peaceful moment in the company of my older son. Even though he is a petulant preteen, even when he is ugly to me, I revel in these rare moments. My cell phone rings.

It's Sharon. We talk about the article, laugh about the $6,000 per month bill that we would have to foot until George was adopted out. She tells me to send George to the ranch or send him back to Romania. I chuckle at the idea, thinking it ridiculous.

Having seen this article, Sharon won't let it go. For months, every telephone conversation with her ends with "Nancy, send him back."

I made the mistake of telling Sharon that our adoption agency offered to abort the adoption. That would mean that George would be sent back into the foster care system he had just come from. Even in my frazzled state, the idea of the horrors George would surely suffer kept me from entertaining that idea. When I start hanging up on Sharon for suggesting that we send George back to Romania, she stops calling.

My closing salvo to her right before hanging up the phone, the comment that ends our twenty-year friendship, is "If you're not going to help me, get out of my way."

Sending George back to Romania would, in my mind, be tantamount to giving him a death sentence. I had seen the Roma, the gypsies in Bucharest, babies no older than George, naked from the waist down, begging in the streets.

When we first met George in Romania, his teeth were rotted through; he needed glasses but had none; his behavior was wild. The idea of this child languishing away in yet another orphanage or, worse yet, on the streets of Bucharest, ending up homeless, soon enough dead, horrified and disgusted me.

Not only that, I reasoned, what would we be teaching Joey by rejecting George? That people are expendable—that when things get tough you just throw inconvenient people away? What do you do when you've been stabbed through the torso by a sword? Do you pull it out or leave it in? Either way, you're a goner.

When I start showing up at book club looking haggard and disinterested, I coincidentally stop getting the e-mails with meeting details. No matter; I had stopped reading the books anyway, so I didn't have anything to add to the discussion. I'd just nod and have a cocktail or two while the smart people talked about plot, character arc, and catharsis.

When our friends only run into me going in or out of the liquor store, they stop inviting us out. No wonder. I look a hundred years old. I can't stand to hear about their little angels' straight A's or which position they're playing in Little League. And I'm tired of complaining about my life. In fact, I'm sick of my own voice.

Pearl S. Buck, the best-selling author of *The Good Earth*, wrote a little book called *The Child Who Never Grew*, half a century before George was even conceived, about her own disabled child, her daughter. When she wrote "People shrink from penetrating surfaces," I knew she was talking about me. Right here, right now, but she wrote it fifty years ahead of time.

Bit by bit, I feel myself falling into a dark empty hole. I was having trouble keeping myself from steering the car into the concrete wall on the side of the highway. The only thing keeping me from it was the thought of my son Joey—in addition to being robbed of a normal childhood, having to deal with the loss of his mother by her own hand.

Once George is on the bus and Joey is on his way to school, I find there is less reason to stay awake. I start to tell myself that, just for today, I'll go back to bed for just a little longer. I'll get myself together by the time Joey walks in the door. I tell myself this so often that, pretty soon, I'm doing the same thing every day. The more I sleep, the more I need to sleep. The same nightmare repeats day after day, night after night. There is a feeling of falling, but it's not me. I look up, and there are my boys, each dangling by the branches of a tree, as far from each other as they can be. I'm racing between them, wondering which will fall first; how do I catch them both?

I have failed at the only thing I'm good at; being a mother is my whole identity. The only piece of me that isn't dead is my connection to Joey, the need to salvage what I can of his childhood. The guilt of stealing his most innocent years to give a home to George eats at me day after day. Giving myself the chance to make up for that is the only thing that gets me out of bed in time to spend the precious little time I have with Joey. On any given school day, we have anywhere from forty-five minutes to an hour and a half between the end of Joey's school day and George's return to the house, when our world collapses.

It would have been easier if somebody died. At least when there's a death, you eventually get over it. Not actually get over it, there is always a wound, but at least the wound scabs over. When you have a child with special needs, they remind you every day that their life will never be what you wanted for them, or for your family. With every sunrise comes a new, darker twilight. The wound never stops bleeding.

CHAPTER 22
HELP! HELP?

Although George went to school, he got kicked out. A lot. As he got older, his classrooms were getting progressively more restrictive, more controlled, more special needs-focused.

The first time I picked George up from school for behavior, I pulled up to the sight of Mrs. O'Rourke carrying a five-year-old tempest, arms flailing, trying to land a punch on his teacher.

Thus began the meetings with the Child Study Team.

My research and the legal credentials after my name scared the staff a little. I was diligent in signing every letter to the board of education with "Esq." following my name. Every time I walked into school, I was greeted with "Yes, Mrs. Thomas, how can we help you?"

I would think "Hell yeah, how can you help me," and then launch into a discussion of the ins and outs of *suck swallow breathe* therapy, an exercise designed to teach George where his tongue was in his mouth so that he could be more intelligible when he talked. I shared with the Child Study Team what I'd learned from Dr. Federici—that while George was in the orphanage, he was probably given a bottle with a huge hole cut into it, to allow for the thick formulaic concoction he was fed to flow freely. In order to keep from choking, George had had to maneuver his tongue to block the flow. Now, as Federici explained, George had no control over where to put his tongue to form words. His teachers looked horrified by this information, their mouths open in dismay, but they had no idea where to begin.

I also embarked on my own research, and would discuss Lindamood-Bell, a teaching method I had read about to help special needs children process information. More blank stares.

The teachers nodded, but nothing changed. The violence was becoming unmanageable. It was overriding his ability to attend school.

As it turned out, the moms of other special needs children would become my best resource.

I met Susan Anderson in the grocery store, wheeling around her twenty-four-year-old catatonic daughter. Susan became my hero. She was a strong advocate for her child at the state level, and, having been at this for so much longer than I, had information and resources to share. I learned a lot from her.

Susan and I had a deal. We seemed to be on similar errand schedules. She never had time to sit down to lunch, and I was just, well, spinning. So, every Tuesday at ten a.m. we would meet in ShopRite, like clockwork. I looked forward to our meetings like I was on my way to the Riviera with a bikini in my bag and my twenty-year-old figure.

During our grocery store meetings, with kindness, patience, and grace, she started to awaken me from my coma of denial. I knew how to research the law, but I couldn't seem to think straight when it came to George; the pounding in my head and the ache in my heart got in the way.

We started simply. The goal of special education is to place students in the least-restrictive environment possible. As George got older and moved from one classroom to the next, each became more restrictive, more self-contained. Soon, we had exhausted every available resource in our district. The board of education knew I wasn't going away, but they didn't want to spend the money to send George out of the school district, to a school dedicated entirely to children with special needs.

Expense is always the bottom line, even though the district is technically not allowed to consider this. They are charged with acting in the best interests of the child. I argued logic; I quoted the law. There is a federal mandate that every child in the country is entitled to a free, appropriate, public education. Where most parents go wrong is pleading that their child isn't reaching their full potential. My friend Susan Anderson taught me more about this, and I was able to zero in on the language in the statute.

The federal school mandate does not dictate that every child must reach their potential—only that they receive an education "appropriate to their needs." I knew that *appropriate* was the key word here, and I used it to my advantage.

When the school district finally relented, George was nine years old. He was little, but he was mighty. And strong. Even though I was trained in protective holds, I always came out of those attempts, to calm George, bruised, sore and sweaty. I'm sure the school district's decision to send George out of district had a lot to do with their concern for lawsuits. He was too strong to handle, and school staff were either unable or unwilling to put themselves in harm's way to calm George's rages. We agreed that George would attend a special needs school that knew how to deal with his outbursts. The school was thirty miles outside the school district, which meant a forty-five-minute bus ride each way, with six hours of school in between. Finally. Five full days of school per week, which meant I would have that time to myself. It sounded heavenly.

George now had a new game: intermittently refusing to get out of bed in the morning, or to brush his teeth, eat breakfast, or get on the bus. Sometimes, he played all the games on the same morning. By the time I got the final warning from the bus driver that she would have to leave if George wasn't out in two more minutes, I was soaking wet from the struggle.

If Joe was home, he would take George's head and I would take his feet, and we would carry George out to the bus, while the bus aide wrestled him into the vest that would ensure he couldn't get out of his seat during the ride.

Sweaty and weak from the violent rage *du jour*, I would trudge back into the house as Joe walked to his car. He would throw over his shoulder, "I could really use your help in the office today" to my deaf ear. I was a battered, exhausted, caffeine-deprived mess.

Sitting on the floor, legs outstretched in front of *The Today Show*, sipping coffee, shaking it off. That's how each day started for me since the advent of Hurricane George. Trying to remember how to breathe.

One day in the frozen food aisle at ShopRite, during one of my weekly meetings with Susan, I was complaining, as usual. Susan had a smile on her face. She was complacent, peaceful, and happy. I thought if I got close enough to her, maybe some of it would rub off on me.

Today I was bemoaning the way I had been berated in the pharmacy. George was already home from school, so I had no choice but to take him with me. He was his usual hugging everybody–touching everything–running away from me, but I needed to pick up my mother's prescription. An old woman was staring at me. With a sneer on her face, she said, "You should make your child behave."

"Seriously?" I shot back. "You can't see that he's disabled?"

"No matter," she threw back at me. "Control your son."

As I'm relaying this story to her, Susan gets a big smile on her face. She pulls me in tight for a bear hug and says, "Oh, Nancy. Aren't we blessed?"

"Are you nuts? How are we blessed?" I'm thinking, *That's it. She's gone over the edge.* I couldn't even imagine what was coming next.

"Because," Susan said, "but for our children, we would be just like those people."

Indeed.

Then, she told me that the Association for Retarded Citizens (ARC) had an after-school program for special needs children. With this kind of support in place, I might have a chance to spend a couple of hours with Joey before George came home.

I made calls to the Department of Human Services and then to ARC, who would tell me that George was number four on the list, then three, then two. I checked in every day for months. One day about six months into the wait, he made it to the top of the list.

When I called Mirlaine, George's caseworker at the Department of Human Services to declare victory and claim his spot, she returned with "Who told you that?"

When I recited my litany to her—quoting the New Jersey statute that stated George was entitled to after-school care, that I knew a spot was open, that George was the next child on the list, and that I knew the name of her supervisor—she had no choice but to e-mail me the paperwork. Before she did, she took one last stab at avoiding fulfilling her job duties: "You realize that you have to fill out a fifty-page form before George can be admitted."

She had the paperwork back in her hands the next morning.

Things went well the first year. George would leave home by 7:30 in the morning, assuming we could wrangle him onto the bus before the bus driver's patience and stopwatch ran out. If there were no violent outbursts, George would leave school and be delivered to after-school care. Then, the bus would bring him home just in time for dinner.

I had taken to having dinner with my son Joey before George walked in the door, so he could be safely ensconced in his room before George blew in. Joe was staying late at the office, so most nights I would put a plate in the oven for him. He would eat whatever dried-out, petrified mess it had turned into by the time he came in, and, as he had watched his dad do for his entire childhood, would always say "Thank you—that was delicious," even if I was no longer in the room and he was saying it to the wall. Most evenings, after picking at what was edible, he would reach for the peanut butter after depositing his plate in the sink.

I tried to leave garlic bread for him most nights so at least he could fill up on something, but for some reason, I had trouble making it. It should be the easiest thing in the world to make, and I always seemed to have stale bread to use up. A little bread, a little butter, a little garlic, and bam, you've got garlic bread, right?

Not always the case.

One morning I woke up to Joe staring out the kitchen window, sipping his coffee.

"Why are there black dots in the snow?"

Man, this guy asked a lot of questions. Didn't he know that if you put the bread in the oven and go, say, to answer the phone, you could maybe forget about garlic bread because one of your friends had had a fight with her boyfriend and had to talk about it right then? Add to that George's mood at the moment the bread is ready to come out of the oven, and a person could lose track of time. And of course, the smoke alarm only goes off when it's too late.

Oh. My. God.

Motherhood is about cooking. And I'm a lousy cook. No wonder I'm a terrible mother.

"Ah, the light dawns."

Shut up, Mom.

By the time George was in bed at night, I was halfway through a bottle of wine and curled up on the sofa with the rest. I hoped to be asleep before Joe came in so he wouldn't notice how much I had drunk before his arrival.

The days had too many waking hours for me; the time spent alone with Joey after school was too short, and the hours spent alone with George, too long. Joe still could not understand why I wasn't practicing law side by side with him. And I couldn't understand why he couldn't see what was happening in our home.

For the four long years since George had come to live with us, I had been trying to get some relief, hoping against hope that my mother would help out. The tumble that Mom took gave me the ammunition for my final, winning salvo.

It was her penchant for complaining that did my mother in.

"You wouldn't believe it. I dropped a glass of water—it slipped right out of my hand. When I bent down to clean it up, my slippers fell out from under me."

Maybe you should have been barefoot, Mom.

"There was glass everywhere, and when I tried to get up, I cut my toe. Then the cabinet door kept swinging away. Every time I would lean on the kitchen cabinet door, it would swing away, and I would fall again. It was three hours before anyone found me."

The thought of my mother grabbing onto the cabinet, thinking she had a grip, leaning up just enough to think she could get her balance, when the door would swing on its hinges, sending her back on her haunches for three solid hours, was more than I could stifle. Since she was uninjured, I let myself enjoy the little comedy. I had to cover the receiver of the phone with my hand to muffle the snorting giggles that came barreling out of me.

Diana, the lady who discovered my mom on the floor that day, lived with her husband in the condo next door. She checked on her frequently, but not on any kind of regular schedule. It was lucky for Mom that Diana happened to pop in when she did.

"That's it. Diana and her husband are moving back to Montana. You have no choice, Mom. Besides, I need your help."

The kind of help my mother rendered was the exact opposite of what I had asked for.

CHAPTER 23
SO CLOSE...

Just when I thought we could manage going on the way we were, George got kicked out of the ARC after-school program. It had only been a year since he started, and I wasn't going to let it end so easily. His offense? He wrestled a two-hundred-pound woman to the ground. It wasn't the first time, or even the second . . . or third. The fourth time. The day had finally arrived when the staff would take no more.

I walked into the ARC center to the sight of a scrawny, fully enraged maelstrom. My son had his caregiver pinned on the floor, her arms over her head to cushion the blows. There was a giant boy in the corner of the room, hands over his ears, rocking to drown out the nightmare he was witnessing.

"I'm sorry, Mrs. Thomas. The safety of our staff is paramount. George will have to go."

I cried. I begged. I promised reform on George's behalf, something I clearly could not deliver. Loving a child with fetal alcohol syndrome is the definition of suspension of disbelief. Nothing makes any sense. The violence would start without warning and end just as unexpectedly. There would be hours of terror, and no memory of it on George's part.

As we made our way to the car, the wild, flailing monster I had come to collect turned into the sedate boy who held my hand and climbed into the backseat for the ride home, saying, "Where now?"

"We're going home, George."

"Why?"

"Honestly, I couldn't tell you."

Trudging to the gallows, I cried the whole ride home.

Now that we were back to shorter days, just school days and back home for George, I had four more hours with George and Joey, at home, together. And Grandma, too.

All the additional stimulation was too much for George, which is how I found myself prone on the floor more often than ever before, George in a protective hold, beads of sweat from my forehead falling on the back of his head, George too embroiled to notice. Following all of the instructions from "The Emperor," I'm whispering in George's ear in dulcet tones, flat affect on my face. "It's okay, George. Calm down. It's okay. Mommy loves you." Only the determination to get past the extinction behavior allows me to ignore the brutality—for those moments, at least.

I knew I was not the target. The nightmares that plagued his little body and memory were the target. The brutality he suffered was the target. The films that played in his head were beyond my worst imagining, and he would never have the words to tell me about them. There was nothing to do but hold him the way I was taught, so he could not hurt himself or seriously injure me.

I knew that if I quit now, this level of fit would mark the threshold for the next one. If I could only hold out until George realized I wasn't going to let him go, there would be relief soon after. I could feel it when he was about to give up. There would be a sigh, and George would take a deep breath. A sign that we were near the end. He would relax in another minute or two, and then I could let him go and he would be on to his next demand.

The way George recovered from his rages was the only blessing; he forgot so quickly that I often questioned whether they had ever happened. But the bruises on my thighs and the pain in my jaw stood as testament, along with my resignation to this death sentence, and my endless need for wine. I would still be getting over the shock to my system, shaking, drinking, checking my latest bruises, while he demanded a snack or TV, repeating his endless mantra of "I want me."

One day, we were approaching the end of one of his rages. I was dripping with sweat, exhausted, and starting to process the latest round of bruises. I always checked for cracked teeth from the backward head butts George was able to manage before I got him in a full protective hold.

Just then, I heard the squeak of my mother's walker as she rounded the corner. In spite of the nonverbal signals I was throwing her, she was heading our way. She ignored my head pointing wildly in the direction from whence she had come, the panic in my eyes.

Finally, I said, "Mom, go back in your room."

My mother was hard of hearing when it suited her. She picked now as one of those times, and kept coming, each squeak of the walker erasing one of the hours I had just put in toward winding down the storm in George. Already hunched from the osteoporosis that made her posture resemble a table, she didn't have far to go to reach down to him, and when she did, she said, "What do you want, George?"

"Mall," he managed to squeak out.

"Oh, George. I want to go to the mall, too."

As Louise turned back to go into her room, I resigned myself to another two hours on the floor with George, a flame reignited in that one short exchange.

Now that George is coming home right after school, Joey and I have even less time together on our own. We experience a new death twice a day: First, when George wakes up and the struggle to get him dressed and on the school bus begins; and second, when the tires of the very same school bus hit the gravel at the top of our fifty-foot driveway. This means that if Joey is home by 2:45 p.m., we have just about an hour to be raucous, and we don't waste a minute.

Joey rarely comes home on the bus. He's complained about the bus ride so many times that I pick him up. Even when I pick him up, he's still complaining, but he's all mine, for the whole car ride, and I can't help but smile while he's ranting about homework… or some kid who stole his sweatshirt. Joey looks at me, annoyance all over his face, "Why are you so happy? Can't you see I'm pissed off?"

I just smile some more, which pisses Joey off some more.

When he enters fifth grade, Joey becomes interested in the sport of fencing. He starts taking lessons every Monday evening. On Tuesday afternoons, he races into the house before I can turn off the car and get inside myself.

With an *En garde!* He tosses me a cooking utensil from the caddy on the kitchen counter. He coaches me through the previous night's lesson, slotted spoon in hand. He teaches me what he's learned about thrusting, or how to keep your target small to your adversary by manipulating your stance. When he runs out of what he knows, he makes it up, and we end up in fits of laughter as I run out of steam.

Inevitably, at the moment that I am about to be stabbed to death by a plastic spatula, we are interrupted by the squeak, squeak, squeak of the wheels of my mother's walker. As she makes her way around the corner, Joey and I freeze, mid-parry with our kitchen utensils. Eyes wide, our silly grins turn to exaggerated expressions of fear, as though we've gotten caught with our hands in the cookie jar.

"Are you Joey's mother or his friend?" Louise asks, arms akimbo.

I never answer. It's less a question than an indictment of my ability to parent.

Throughout my childhood, my mother reminded me that it was her job to be my mother, never my friend. She fulfilled her own prophecy, but I would not allow her to fulfill the same one for me.

Joey's interests are varied, and he also loves oceanography, which is a relief to me. I had no idea what I was doing with an épée / slotted spoon in my hand; our bouts always ended with my submitting to his greater skill in favor of avoiding certain defeat. When I think about it, the best part of surrendering was hearing my son utter *Touché* as he sauntered away.

There is much less required of me during Joey's exploration of the ocean. I drive him to Barnes & Noble and finance the building of his impressive library of naval history and sea life. We watch as much of *National Geographic's Ocean Life* series as we can get in before four p.m. Watching fish breed and feed requires a more sedate and passive contribution on my part. As Joey's room fills with books, I happily order another book-case, and then another. A small token for the bits of peace I can provide in his world. I soak up as much Joey as I can until the arrival of George's bus marks the end of our frivolity.

I press the button and, as the garage door rises, it makes a grinding sound that reminds me of the rack, the torture machine that stretches its victims, a staple of many horror movies. It needs to be greased but never is, just more evidence of life falling down around me.

At my insistence, Joey flies up the stairs to his bedroom before George can catch sight of him, where he'll be safely ensconced for homework, or TV, or computer time, oblivious to the battle that will rage until I call him for dinner, George safely fed, washed up, and asleep.

CHAPTER 24
ESCAPE ARTISTRY IN THREE EASY STEPS

Once I realized that my husband Joe was never going to cut the apron strings he clung to so tightly, I gave up trying to make our relationship look like a marriage. That included having an exit plan. A few years after the wedding, I purchased a condo in a little town in Florida called Hobe Sound. Sharon had found it, and it fit in with our plan to spend our friendship together in the Sunshine State. It was one of those moments when Joe had nodded, and I pounced. My mom had given me the down payment, so Joe couldn't argue much when I told him that it was a good investment and that we could rent it out and cover the cost of the mortgage. Letting me buy that condo shut me up for a few years. But the years went on, and Joe wasn't making any motions toward moving. Joe would always listen politely enough when I prattled on about wanting us to move there. I'd found a private school for Joey near the condo, support and special education for George, and now I had a place for us to stay in the summer when the golf pros I rented to every winter left.

My husband let it slip that he wasn't interested in moving to Florida with me, even though he had allowed me to labor under the pretense that my desires mattered to him.

One night in a moment of weakness, he said, "I'll never leave New Jersey while my parents are alive."

I started making my own retirement plans.

Joe's family has longevity in its bloodline. His parents were still youngish, in their early seventies. No one in his family died until they were in their nineties. (To my mind, twenty years was too long to wait to start living.) I think the secret to their old age was that they never retired; they just fell over in their offices.

Secretly, I began calling the condo my *Screw you* house. This was because I now knew for sure that one day, I would leave Joe and fulfill my dream of living in Florida, but I would be moving there by myself. I would become an eccentric old lady, surrounded by felines, picking up seashells along the beach.

My romantic life with my husband was over. As I lost respect for him, my desire waned until it disappeared completely. Ever the optimist, he accepted my rejection of him, though he never stopped trying. I believed that I would never again have love in my life. If I couldn't have physical pleasure, I could at least have pets. "Crazy Cat Lady" seemed like a noble aspiration.

Every time we took a vacation to Florida, I used the summer camp at the Florida Association for Retarded Citizens (ARC) to give George as much of a camp experience as he could absorb, and to give the rest of us the chance to relax. As long as they were willing, for a small stipend per day, George would be entertained, managed, taken to water parks, and supervised, leaving Joe, Joey and me to loll on the beach, go fishing, relax. Sometimes, this ARC would let me hire some of their employees to babysit George after camp. It was a great trade. George got to commandeer the remote control and stay up late, and the rest of us got to go to dinner.

It was two weeks of heaven in the summer, punctuated by small bouts of Hurricane George twice a day. I thought I had it all figured out for a couple of summers, until George wore out his welcome.

Just as he had done at the after-school program, George would rage. He would be asked to comply, or wait his turn, or hang up his backpack when he didn't want to do it. He would take down someone bigger than himself. He would endanger the staff. Consequently, he was barred from attending the camp.

One summer after George had lost his ticket to the ARC in New Jersey and his ticket to summer camp in Florida, I had an idea.

My mother moved in with us four years after George did. Not only was Louise never afraid of George, but George had never acted out to her. Not once. I left them alone together often, for short periods, to run an errand our go to the grocery store. George would just sit on the floor next to my mother, and watch TV with her. When she got tired of him playing with the buttons that lifted her out of her electric recliner, she would just hand over the remote for a little peace.

The violence never touched Grandma. Maybe their souls had made a deal on the lawn of heaven before they arrived on Earth. They say the Lord protects widows and orphans. They were bookends, and maybe that's why my mother was not afraid of him. She had no need to be.

I thought that if I could leave George in my mother's care for a couple of weeks, we could take our summer vacation as planned.

Occasionally, my mother would even take George to TGI Fridays or Chili's. I was always on call, just in case. For the hour and a half it took them to get two miles down the road, have dinner, and come home, George was pretty manageable. He knew that he was having a treat, that if he wanted to go, he needed to behave. And he did the best that he could. Hugging strangers was a problem, but seeing this oddly inappropriate child with a hunched-over, gray-haired old lady seemed to soften people, and he got away with a lot more than he did when he was in public with me.

One night when George was particularly compliant, and they had had their little "date," my mom said, "Funny, George is good when I'm alone with him."

She was right. And she was around for a lot of the meltdowns. In fact, whenever George wanted to taunt his brother, he would hide behind my mother. He would stick his tongue out and call his brother "mean lady," or "You stupid," and run behind my mother's chair. Grandma was the safe haven.

My plan was coming together. I laid a trap for her, and my mother walked right into it. "Mom, we need a vacation," I said. "What do you think about babysitting George while we go to Florida?"

Before she could protest, without taking a breath, I continued. "Besides, my in-laws are ten minutes away if you need help. I'm sure they will take him whenever you need them to," I lied. "George goes to school during the summer. All you have to do is get him off the bus, let him watch TV as much as he wants, feed him, and let him sleep wherever he wants."

I was beyond caring about whether George had discipline or a routine. I needed a break.

The extended school year program—the summer session put in place for special needs children by the school district—helped me seal the deal. For six weeks during the summer, the children went to school, just like during the year. We would take our vacation during the extended school year. My mother reluctantly agreed, and I went into full Florida vacation planning mode.

Life was good. For two full days Joey and I played dolphins and sharks in the community pool while Joe sunbathed and napped. Whether I was the dolphin or the shark, Joey thought that the point of the game was to drown me. I didn't care. I had my son's attention and I reveled in it. Joey was carefree, fun, and funny. Gasping for breath was a good trade, a price I gladly paid.

On the morning of our third day in Florida, the phone rang in the condo. No one knew this number but salespeople and my mother.

"You have to come home," my mom managed to get out between gasping for air. "I have shingles."

I said, "Mom, we can't come home. Our flight isn't until the twelfth. What do you want me to do?"

"Come home. I'm sick. The doctor said it's from stress. George is driving me crazy. He won't listen to me. He does whatever he wants. He's sleeping in the closet. Your in-laws don't answer the phone. I need you."

I feigned surprise, even though none of it surprised me.

What followed was a flurry of phone calls between Joe and his mom, and plane reservations were made.

In a few days, we were back in New Jersey. Now I was nursing my mother, running to the pharmacy and fielding phone calls to her doctor, in between the storm that was George, and entertaining Joey in the crevices of time that remained for him. Listening to Louise rail about how we had abandoned her with a wild child took all the vacation out of me. I resented her. I resented everybody.

Until the day she died, my mother would remind me of the angry red rash, the itching and the searing pain that plagued her for years after the original illness passed. She loved to research her ailments and all the potential side effects of her medications. The amazing thing about being a hypochondriac is that you seem to be able to produce symptoms on demand. Once my mother learned about postherpetic neuralgia—the severe pain that can last for months or even years in the area of the healed rash—and learned how to pronounce it, she would tell anyone who stood still long enough all about it. And how it was my fault.

One day, at the end of my rope, I said, "Mom, you've got to stop complaining. Can't you say anything positive?"

Without taking a breath, she answered, "I'm not complaining. I'm just telling you what's wrong."

Since you put it that way, Mom, carry on.

In the meantime, I had bought myself a car. Actually, I had Joe buy it. Ford had just introduced a three-row sport utility vehicle, and it had a video player in it. This car was longer than most SUVs, and the third row, where George would sit, was spacious. Most importantly, it was farther away from me, the driver, than the others I had seen.

It was time for a new car. The Mercedes station wagon that I loved driving had given us its last breath. It was a new car or a new engine for the old one. We decided on a new car, and I convinced Joe to buy me this one. Secretly, I knew that if I put George in the third row and he was having a bad day, he couldn't hurt me from all the way back there. George had been issued a special restraint from the board of education for when he rode the school bus. It prevented George from letting himself out.

With no small amount of cajoling, begging and, finally, threats of lawsuits if George got hurt in the car or hurt one of us, I had been issued one, too. It wouldn't stop the screaming or the kicking, but it kept George in his seat. I would have a fighting chance to get home, or at least to find somewhere safe to pull off the road and let his rage run its course.

What I told Joe was that I liked the way it drove, the video player would keep the kids occupied on long trips, and it had lots of room. This was all true.

If I had told him the primary reason—that I thought I needed the third row for my own safety—I would have had to admit that George was a danger to us.

The reality I faced was the last thing I wanted for my life, my family, or my future.

CHAPTER 25
MOMMY DEAREST

My father died unexpectedly when I was sixteen years old, leaving Mom a widow at the age of fifty-three. The day my father died was the day my mother forgot how to live. My mother, Louise, became headstrong, independent, and single-minded. And a little bitter.

We were in Washington, DC, looking at colleges, when it happened. I was a young high school junior, and was set to graduate high school and start college at the age of seventeen. We had planned the tour for spring. Easter break would be a perfect time to see the cherry blossoms. My father loved to "take a ride," especially on Sundays after church, before the relatives would show (or not show) up for Sunday dinner. This trip was just an extended Sunday-morning ride. He loved to take in new sights, and road trips were his way to connect us as a family, to show us the world. My mother always had fruit and cheese in a plastic bag, in case anybody got hungry, and napkins, so we wouldn't mess up the car seats.

And there was my dad. "Louise, why isn't she looking out the window? Nancy, look out the window. There's so much to see."

I didn't mind listening to eight-tracks of Jerry Vale, but much to my father's frustration, I was already seeing everything I wanted, wrapped up in my favorite authors, all in the backseat with me. I hated car rides, but I wanted to be near my father. Besides, staying home was not an option. No self-respecting Italian daddy would ever let his daughter stay home with babysitters. They were strangers, and, in my protective father's eyes, the world was full of evil people in an evil world. He was here to protect us.

My father worked outside in the weather, year-round, as a scrap metal dealer. He couldn't bear to be in school, and had an entrepreneurial spirit. He didn't want that life for me. I was going to college, even though he had quit school in the fourth grade to deliver ice in the Bronx, back in the day when people had iceboxes.

When my father bought his business in Bridgeport it was called Tommy's Junk Shop. Even after he changed the name to Ferraro Brothers, people were still looking for Tommy. Some Saturday mornings, he would take me to work with him, and I would answer the phone. When somebody called for Tommy, I'd press the intercom and announce to my dad that he had a call.

He worked hard, but my father also played, and when he did, he took us with him. He loved to fly to warm places in the winter and didn't hesitate to pull me out of school to do it, promising my teachers that the homework they supplied would be done and handed in when I returned. Lucky for us, my grades were high, so my teachers couldn't argue. In hindsight, I have no doubt that there might have been some cash exchanged for letting us break the rules. Because when my mother asked, she was always told no. Somehow, when my father showed up to talk to my teachers, he always came back with approval.

My father was the indisputable head of our household. When my mother even suggested getting a part-time job as a hobby, you would have thought she'd killed somebody.

"My wife will not work," he said. "Do you want people to think I can't support my family?"

So, my mother stayed home until the day my father died. And cooked. And cleaned. She cleaned so much that she invented new patterns in the plush rust-colored carpet that covered our living and dining rooms, so she could tell if you walked on it. In our small ranch house, the living and dining rooms easily took up a third of our living quarters.

"Get off my rug" was yelled at me so many times that I had invented a way to get to the upright piano that stood against the wall without disturbing the pattern. You had to stand on tiptoe, and if you got to the bench with your butt first and swung your legs around to the rug remnant which was wedged under the pedals—which, by the way, matched the rest of the carpeting—you could save yourself from having to re-vacuum the room so the pattern all matched. No wonder I hated having to practice the piano—it was dangerous, because it potentially involved housework. I was a good sight reader, which meant that I could slack on the practice and make up for it by the seat of my pants, so my piano teachers thought I practiced more than I did.

One day, my mother's mother, Carolina (inspiration for my love of the name "Caroline"), a woman I adored, accompanied me to piano lessons. I took my place on the piano bench. She sat quietly in the corner in her simple but perfectly pressed shift, her large frame uncomfortable on the only other seat in the room, a metal folding chair. Her face was pink, perfectly setting off her pure white hair. Her cheeks reminded me of cherubs. When my piano teacher, Mr. LoPinto, commented on what a good job I did and how I must have practiced a lot that week, my grandma piped up in her broken English, "Oh, she-a no practice."

I didn't talk to my beloved grandmother for a week, the very same woman who would stand at my mother's stove to make my farina just the way I liked it: lumpy, with a cracked egg in the middle. And sugar sprinkled on top. Still, a week of silence.

On Sundays, all bets were off. After church and maybe a ride or a visit to Aunt Lilly's house in Bridgeport for a cuppa coffee and a biscotti, my daddy would call me into the living room. He would read me the "funny papers," the color comics that came with the Sunday edition of the *Bridge-port Post*, sitting there on my mother's formal sofa, his stocking feet on her precious marble coffee table. He made up the dialogue between Sarge and Beetle Bailey, but I didn't care. Being close to the man who thought I could do no wrong, my first hero and protector, was priceless to me. Even after I learned to read, and knew he was making up the words, I would sit, rapt, listening to him read me the funny papers.

After that, it was time to play the piano.

"Play me a song, *bella*."

No matter how many sour notes I hit, my daddy always told me it was the sweetest music he'd ever heard. We ate in the dining room, and I got a splash of Egri Bikavér, my dad's favorite wine, in my 7UP. *Bull's Blood.* The label had a large black bull on it, in full charging stance. It came from Hungary, but we ignored that minor detail. You can't drink a more masculine wine than that.

My mother never said a word. She wasn't allowed. But her skin was crawling. A woman who ironed the sheets before she put them on the bed. That was Louise. On Mondays, as soon as my father was off to work, my mother would vacuum the dining and living rooms, mop the floors, Windex everything that stood still until it had no choice but to shine. On Mondays, the whole house smelled like Lysol. To this day the smell of that disinfectant makes my stomach turn. But you could eat off her floors. And God help you if you left a dirty fork in the sink. She made order out of her world and kept it that way all week. Until Sunday.

I was a good girl, even by the time we got to DC to look at colleges. I was still a good girl, but I was a teenager, petulant and hormonal. Disrespectful speech was not allowed toward adults, especially my parents. My father only slapped me once. It wasn't the act that crushed me. It was the disappointment in his eyes, and the way he held a grudge. After three weeks of sulking in my room, my mother finally spoke up to him. "If she gets sick, Henry, it will be your fault."

She was good at guilt. Italian mothers are like that. He somehow forgave me, but neither of us ever wanted that to happen again, so instead of talking back, I hid in my room, emerging long enough for dinner, making a quick escape under the pretense of homework. I hid in my room so much that when Helen Reddy released the song "Leave Me Alone," my dad brought the record home and played it over and over on the record player in the basement, turning up the volume so I could hear it from my bedroom. My new theme song. He also brought home the sheet music and made me play it for him on the piano. It replaced the other song he

loved to play for me, Sinatra singing "Nancy (With the Laughing Face)."
I preferred the latter, so I forced myself to stop sulking and attempt to
act like an actual civilized human. No small feat for a hormonal, moody,
pubescent teenage girl.

When we got to Washington, my dad dropped us off at Catholic
University. It was a long drive, and he wanted to go back to our hotel
to take a nap—what would be his last—while my mother and I toured
the campus. Words of affection didn't come easily to me then. I thought
saying "I love you" to your parents was weird and embarrassing, so when
those words, "I love you, Daddy," came out of my mouth, I was startled.
I didn't know then that those were the last words I would ever speak to
him while he was alive.

I also shocked myself a little when I found myself in the Basilica of
the National Shrine of the Immaculate Conception, the church on the
grounds of Catholic University, kneeling before the shrine to Mary, the
mother of God, reciting the prayer I had spoken since I could talk. "Hail
Mary, full of grace," it started. Tears started to flow, but I didn't know
why—until we returned to our hotel room. We found my father in bed.
He looked like he was asleep, a spaghetti Western with John Wayne, his
favorite actor of all time, on the TV. Except he wouldn't wake up.

The bedding was undisturbed. The only blessing. At the age of sixty-
one, he had died in his sleep.

We found out later from Dr. Cooper that my dad had known he was
dying. He knew he needed open heart surgery to treat his atherosclerosis,
hardening of the arteries. This was before angioplasty, the much less inva-
sive and safer alternative, was invented, but it wouldn't have mattered.
My father, just like his brothers, didn't trust doctors, didn't like them.
They were afraid of doctors. Just the way the Portokalos family in *My
Big Fat Greek Wedding* used Windex to cure everything, our family had a
panacea. If you didn't feel well, you had a little red wine and a meatball. If
that didn't work, you took a little Brioschi, the Italian version of antacid,
and went to church. You put the money in the box, lit a candle, and said
a novena to your patron saint. *Finito.*

My sister's family was an hour away from us. She had two small children, which kept her busy and unable to give my mother all the attention she wanted. With just the two of us in the house now, my mother had nothing to focus on but cooking, cleaning, and me. Since her house was always immaculate, she lasered in on me.

Louise used my father's death in DC against me. She told me that it was my father's dying wish that I not attend Catholic University. It was too far away, it was too dangerous, and besides, she had promised. There's a special place in hell for Catholics, especially Italian Catholics, who go against a dying declaration, so instead, I enrolled in Fairfield University.

Fairfield was only fifteen minutes away from our home in Trumbull, and I commuted to class and came home at night. I bugged her so much that by the second semester, my mother let me move into the dorms, to "have the experience." As it turned out, "the experience" included her showing up unannounced to argue with me or see what I was doing when I was out from under her thumb. She showed up so often that I ran out of places to hide when my one of my floormates would yell down the hall, "Nancy, your mom's here . . . again."

I moved back home. It wasn't worth the embarrassment.

It didn't help that the day I moved to campus was also the day my boyfriend Caesar broke up with me. Up until that time, we had been a perfect Italian couple. He was from a respectable family, I was always in by curfew, and my mother liked him. He was only twenty-one years old, but Caesar had a closet full of three-piece suits. Whenever we walked into any Italian restaurant in New Haven a chorus would go up. "*Cesare. Vieni qui.*"

On weekends, Caesar would parade me into the living room of his parents' home and seat me at their white lacquer grand piano with gold gilt trim, to play "Für Elise" for his family and their visitors. They were grooming him for a Senate seat, and I was a perfect mate. A naive, smart, pretty, Italian girl who looked good on his arm. He never touched me, except for a peck on the lips. It wouldn't have been appropriate.

But now, I was tainted by the sin of living on campus. There was no telling what I was doing. With the loss of Caesar as my boyfriend, I was no longer worthy of being a respectable Italian wife. *Fanculo.* Fucked.

CHAPTER 26
COOKING . . . NOT FOR THE MEEK

I'm standing at the stove, pretending to cook.

A few months after my mother moved in with us, I had to stop letting her cook in my home. She had been preparing meals since she moved in, and they were delicious. But at every physical exam, Joey is always in the 120th percentile for weight, when measured against children his age. Even though he's tall and in the 90th percentile for height, his pediatrician complains that he's not growing fast enough to support his appetite, and he tends toward the lazy side. Couple that with his penchant for arguing with me over everything, especially what he ate; when I try directing him toward fruit or, God forbid, a cucumber, it's World War III.

There is no arguing my mother's culinary skills, but when I watch her fry the meatballs I loved so much as a child, and, instead of throwing away the grease it produces, pouring it into her saucepot, I have to put my foot down.

One day, watching her perform her delicious, deadly ritual, I snapped. "Mom, for God's sake. You killed your husband with this shit. You can't kill my family too."

She never again lit my stove. And she never let me live down that insult.

So now, I'm back to cooking dinner. But I have a cookbook. A cookbook that promotes sneaking vegetables into a child's diet. When I make my tomato sauce, I add chickpeas. You're not supposed to be able to tell.

Nobody is happy.

I'm stirring fast, so the pureed beans will melt into the sauce before anyone else can see. The whole thing turns orange, but I tell myself no one will notice once it's on the rice pasta that nobody likes. The last time I checked, two plus two still made four, but I've convinced myself that if you put a few relatively putrid ingredients together, sis-boom-bah, you can make something delicious. Palatable. Edible. Maybe.

I'm stirring, furiously now, because I can hear the boys approaching, and don't want to give Joey the opportunity to say, "Ewww, Mom. I'm calling Dad to bring home a pizza."

Now that Louise is in the house, things aren't necessarily better, but I think there might be a shift in the atmosphere. About the time I reclaimed the cooking duties, stirring some concoction and standing at the stove, I can't believe what I'm witnessing. George is now eight, Joey is ten. Except for one time when my husband flew kites with the boys, they have never been able to enjoy time with each other. After years of my trying in vain to make them compatible, my two boys are crawling on the floor together, laughing and racing Tonka trucks through the living room, under the piano, around the kitchen table, finally crashing into my sneakers. A miracle has occurred, and I don't dare move my feet, or complain, or react. My children are bonding. They are playing together. Finally. I'm starting to think the combination of all of us under the same roof, my mother, my boys and me, just might give us enough grace to get through this.

They move on past the kitchen to my mother's room, where Louise is pouting. *The Price is Right* is blaring on her TV. They zoom their way in, and then suddenly, silence.

Joey emerges, shaking his head.

"Joey, what happened?" I ask.

No answer as he stomps up the stairs. I hear his bedroom door slam as George enters the kitchen, his Tonka truck in pieces in his hand.

"Grandma. Mean lady."

"Mom, what the heck?" I'm screaming at my mother. "They were playing together. They were laughing. They were happy. What the hell happened?"

"They were bothering me" was her only response as she turned her head back toward the game show.

Fanculo. Fucked again.

I pour a glass of wine while I plan her murder. And then another glass while I talk myself down from certain jail time.

CHAPTER 27
I WANT ME, TOO

I'm in the family room, just trying to have a normal Tuesday afternoon, as unrealistic an idea as that had become, playing referee to my now thirteen- and eleven-year-old boys.

My mother had been living with us for three years now. Her room was in the back of the house, off the garage. As the years passed, she came out of her bedroom less and less. Combined with her real hearing loss and her selective hearing loss, Louise could always claim ignorance of the fracas going on around us.

"No, George. No *Cops*. Too violent. How about Xbox Bowling," I plead, trying to placate the two boys thrown together without their consent. In an attempt at conventionality Joey takes the controls and starts the game, intent on the next strike.

The waiting proves too much for George. His angelic face twists into fury, and he screams, "I want me, I want *me*, I WANT ME," George-speak for "my turn." His only means of communicating his wants, needs, and desires, one of the few three-word sentences at his disposal, one of the few sentences that make sense of his world.

"Okay, George. You can have a turn. Just wait a minute."

"I want me, I want *me*, I WANT ME," it continues.

"Mom, make him stop. I mean it." Joey's fuse is short.

But there is no making George stop. George is losing it, and in a few short moments, Joey is, too.

Thirteen-year-old Joey flings the controller across the room, in the direction of George's head. It whizzes by his left ear, a narrow miss.

"Here you go, asshole, your turn," Joey spits, and stomps up the stairs, abusing the treads with his already-six-foot linebacker frame, throwing his full weight against the walls on his way.

The "I want me" desires presumably fulfilled, George is now in charge of the controller.

But the child is not placated. Sarcasm is not lost on this little boy, even with the depth of his challenges. He spits out his other favorite phrase, "Mean lady," after the hulking male frame, giving chase.

Under any other circumstances, it would be funny—the idea of a burly teenage boy, almost a man, being called something so utterly ridiculous and feminine. But it only incenses the kid who longs for a normal five minutes, any five minutes, in his own home.

Joey's tirade is just beginning.

"I want him gone by Saturday," he shrieks from the top of the stairs, and I think *So do I*, but dare not let the thought escape my lips.

In full pursuit of his brother, George's feet barely touch the floor as he flies up the stairs, attempting engagement with Joey. I chase after both boys, hoping to catch George before the inevitable conflict. I reach him, and the full force of George's firestorm is unleashed on me. The protective holds, hours, days of training from experts in calming the rage of Hurricane George, all goes out the window as I attempt to deflect one punch after another. Some land, but I do not feel them until much later, my only thought to keep George out of his brother's line of fire.

Meanwhile, the full extent of Joey's wrath and frustration is gathering steam in the crash of his most treasured possessions. Joey smashes the crystal sailfish against the wall. The sound of it shattering takes the top left corner of my heart with it. It is followed by the rest of his precious collection of Oceania, five years of curating. The crystal octopus sculpture is next, the one for which he begged, and cost so much more than I wanted to pay. I begin to raise my voice in protest, but the words catch in my throat. I say nothing. I have no right.

It takes superhuman strength; I don't know from where it comes. I wrestle George into the third row of my new SUV, and attach the restraint that he has not yet figured out how to open. I finally get him in with a mixture of brute force and the promise of a visit to Wawa, the convenience store that's Disneyland for coffee lovers. And George loves coffee. Almost as much as he loves his temper. But he screams the whole trip, kicking the back of the seat in front of him and throwing punches. He's not used to being so far away from the driver's seat, and he looks surprised when his punches don't land.

I pull over, waiting for the storm to pass. Twenty minutes later and I am still parked on the shoulder of the road. I stand outside the car, waiting for the rage to run its course. Cars pass, their occupants oblivious to the human tempest who is tearing up the inside of my brand-new car. A police cruiser. I look up expectantly. But he doesn't stop. A fire truck; no response. I'm torn between flagging them down and waiting out the typhoon contained in the metal box on wheels behind me. What would I say? How could I explain this? How would George be treated at the hands of strangers?

So, I wait for the explosion that has taken the place of my child to wear itself out. As quickly as it began, it's over. George has exhausted himself, and is now sitting up in his seat, looking expectantly at the crazy woman who promised him coffee. I drive to Wawa, somehow steering through silent sobs, relief at having prevented one more violent fraternal conflict, discounting the cost to my well-being as the price of motherhood.

Coffee in hand, George is finally mollified, "Sorry, sorry, sorry, Mommy" on his lips.

But the words have no meaning for him. To George, they are simply the bridge back to his world, a world where he demands and receives. There's no point in talking to George about it. He wouldn't understand anyway. I steer the car into the driveway, partially relieved at having kept Joey from pummeling George, but mostly full of dread. What would I find when I walked in the door?

I seat George in the family room, remote control in his hand.

"Here, George, enjoy *Cops*."

Joey is still barricaded in his room. Although he refuses to answer, I satisfy myself that he has done no irreparable damage to himself or the dog. I tiptoe past the family room, where the autistic–fetal alcohol syndrome–attachment disorder–bipolar–sotted child sips his pumpkin decaf latte and vicariously experiences the adventures of the violent and those who would stop them. Picking up tips for the next rage, no doubt.

Right now, I am beyond caring about tomorrow. I'm just trying to get through today.

It's only three o'clock in the afternoon, but I think, "Hell, it's five o'clock somewhere," and make my way to the pantry to uncork a bottle of red table wine. And then another. Always prepared, I have laid in a goodly supply, lest there be a shortage of grapes. The rich merlots I used to enjoy have given way to buying in bulk, but I barely notice, enjoyment of the vintage not my primary goal.

And now I have a new skill. I found a way to uncork a bottle of wine without a corkscrew. I had read online that if you put a shoe against the wall and slammed the bottom of the bottle into it, it would knock out the cork. I tried it. It worked. It worked well. And it was a lot faster than fishing for a corkscrew in the bottom of the junk drawer. Life wasn't okay, but I had wine, the numbing elixir that got me through the interminable afternoons with George and made me invisible to my husband.

Just as the bruises are starting to rise and the bump on my knee is starting to throb, the numbing sensation takes over and envelops me in a foggy blanket of woe. The wine grants permission for the tears to flow but won't wash away the guilt of robbing one son's childhood to give one to another, the dread of the next rage, the regret for poor decisions made and the anger I am not allowed to express. For now.

CHAPTER 28

WHAT DO YOU CALL A WHALE WATCH WITH NO WHALES?

It was like my friend Susan was psychic. Or maybe when we met in the grocery store I just looked so haggard and when she called to check on me I sounded so drained that she knew I wasn't getting any relief.

She had started calling me weekly to check on my progress. When she sensed I was ready to wave my white flag, she suggested we try the hotel respite program.

"Nancy, if you register for respite care, George will be entitled to thirty days a year."

"What is this magical respite of which you speak?" I said. I couldn't believe my ears.

"There are group homes all over the state. The staff are qualified, trained to deal with people like George. It's so the rest of the family can take a break. They even have weekend outings in hotels so the children can swim. You can use it all at once or spread it out."

Not convinced, I had her tell me more.

"The children go on outings, to zoos and to baseball games," Susan continued. "Sometimes they even stay at hotels and use the pools there. The caregivers are highly trained and screened. The kids love it. It's like they're on vacation, too. Check it out."

She gave me some names and phone numbers of providers, and I was off.

Mirlaine was the caseworker assigned to George at the State Division of Developmental Disabilities. We had first met on the phone when I had submitted my initial registration paperwork.

The day she called to introduce herself, butter wouldn't have melted in her mouth. Mirlaine listened politely while I described my typical day. She clucked at the diagnoses I had just received and said that she understood. We ended the conversation with her saying "I will do everything I can to help you."

When I called to speak to Mirlaine about the respite program, I got her voicemail, which always ended with "Have a blessed day." Okay.

Two days went by. Then three. I started to talk back to "Have a blessed day," and hanging up, I would mutter to myself "Have a blessed day, my ass."

That is how I started my letter-writing campaign to Mirlaine. She had made the mistake of providing me a copy of their Family Support Mission Statement, and I quoted it back to her, including the language about the respite program providing out-of-home services in hotels, and in-home services to give temporary relief to families from caregiving. We were entitled to thirty hours a month of in-home services and thirty days per year of out-of-home services. Mirlaine especially disliked it when I repeated our telephone conversations in writing and copied her supervisors. Before I discovered the missing magical piece of information, which granted us those thirty days a year. I had been using respite services, but infrequently and for short periods of time. I would beg, I would cry, and I would be granted a few hours a month, so that we could go out to dinner or try to take Joey on an outing. I thought I was getting help because Mirlaine took pity on our family. In truth, she was holding out on me, and I went after all those missing days of help with a vengeance.

This started a cycle of getting information on new respite programs from Susan, calling the program for information and availability, and then writing to Mirlaine with all the information I had gleaned. She had no choice but to help me; I was relentless. When it became easier for her to actually perform her job rather than ignore my constant requests, we came to terms. She stopped asking me how I found out about particular programs, and I stopped copying her bosses on my letters.

Joey's romance with everything ocean ran deep. I did everything I could to encourage his interests. I felt I owed it to him.

Cape May in the summer is a wondrous place for a boy who loves the ocean. The southernmost tip of New Jersey, it's the only place in the state to see the sun rise and set on the water in the same day.

During one of my weekly grocery store check-ins with Susan, she mentioned a respite home not far from Cape May. If I could get George in for a weekend, I could take Joey there. We would go on a whale watch and then to Sunset Beach to watch the sunset while "Taps" played and the American flag was lowered with the sun. Meanwhile, we wouldn't be far from the respite home just in case George needed us.

I conducted my due diligence, secured George's place, and wrote my letter to Mirlaine. We went. We had had the occasional respite weekend, but had never ventured away from home while George was away for the weekend. The respite home was what we had come to expect from our prior, shorter bursts of relief. The furnishings were simple and the walls were bare. Sensory stimulation is kept to a minimum in an effort to maintain calm. George was happy to go, because he is always ready to explore new places and accept services from anyone who is not me.

We went on our whale watch, but there were no whales. It was just a great ride on the waves, breathing salty air and watching the dolphins race alongside our boat. Joey and I were munching on lobster rolls, getting fortified for a long swim in the ocean. The summer encased us, caressed us with its warm breeze, and the sun was shining on our already sunburned faces, when my cell phone rang.

All I could hear was George crying. His caregiver was yelling into the receiver over the background noise. "Mrs. Thomas, George is having a difficult time here. One of the other guests had an incident. George didn't react well. If we can't calm him down, perhaps you should come and get him."

I couldn't bear to spoil this moment for Joey.

"If you like," she continued, "I will call you back in an hour. George might be all right by then."

I had the phone pressed close to my ear, but the cacophony was so loud that Joey heard every word.

"Mom," he said, "we should go get him."

When we arrived at the home, a young girl, about twelve years old, was still in distress. She was moaning and tearing at her clothes. This had put George in distress. Without any coping skills, George had melted down, too.

The ride home was two hours of terror. George could not be calmed. The only thing to do was to pull the car over and let his storm run its course. Except the storm wouldn't end. Cars were whizzing by us on the two-lane road that led in and out of town. They whizzed by so fast and so close to us that our car shook when each one passed. It was too dangerous to drive with George in this condition, but it was too dangerous to sit on the side of this road, as well.

As George kicked, screamed, cried and threw punches in the air, I drove carefully back onto the road, blocking him out of my mind as best I could. I remember yelling to Joey, trying to make small talk, in spite of the tempest in the backseat. We made it home, but I don't remember the trip.

A few days later, I was strolling through ShopRite, relishing the relative quiet and cool air. George was in the extended school year program, and Joey was at home in the family room. It was a sunny summer day and we needed groceries.

In no particular hurry, I was comparing nutrition information on two different cereals. Joey wanted Froot Loops; I wanted him to eat Cheerios. George's latest tantrum was still weighing on me, Joey's abbreviated trip to the shore disturbing.

I settled on Froot Loops as my cell phone rang.

"Mom, where are you?" asked Joey.

"Honey, I'm in the grocery store. What's wrong?"

"Mom-Mom's here," he answered. "She's been here a long time."

When I walk into the house, my mother-in-law had steam coming from her ears.

"I didn't know you were coming over," I said, as nonchalantly as I could manage, but her head was shaking. Something was coming. Muriel had been sitting on my couch for the past hour, with Joey, questioning him about the weekend in Cape May. He had told her, in what I could only imagine was a dramatic rendition with visuals, his impressions of the respite home and what we found there when we went to pick up George.

"What did you do to my grandson?" Muriel asked. "You took him to that awful place where people were running wild, and you exposed him to that? How dare you?"

"How dare I?" I sputtered.

She had broken the dam, and I wasn't measuring my words. I pulled myself up to my full height and invaded her space, leaning in so she could feel my breath when I spit at her.

"How dare I? Where were you? Where was everybody when I was sitting at the table with Joey trying to do his homework? Where was everybody when George was beating me up? Not one of you ever offered to take George for an hour, or even to drive him through McDonald's. I need help. We have a disabled child on our hands, and not one of you cares."

Joe's extended family consisted of three grown sisters, all with their own families. His parents lived fifteen minutes down the road. Except for Lynda, the baby of the family, and her husband Peter, everyone else lived within a ten-mile radius of our home. Even though we had asked, no one was willing to take George without one of us present, even for an hour or two.

As Muriel stormed out the door, she threw back at me, "I had no idea."

Well, she did now.

But nothing changed.

CHAPTER 29
MY HEART SKIPPED A BEAT

The kids were out of the house for the day, and Mommy Dearest was in her room, pouting over some lack of attention, not enough trips to the mall, my cooking, while Joe's constant plaint, "Why aren't you in the office helping me?" echoes against the walls of my brain.

The only answer I could come up with, at that moment, was "Because I can't even remember my own name."

In the shower, my chest started to heave. I couldn't catch my breath and my arms went numb. I thought of calling 911 but think better of it. If my mother saw an ambulance pull into the driveway, not to be outdone, she would feign some emergency and end up on the stretcher next to me on the way to the hospital.

On the day I gave birth to Joey Matthew, a planned cesarean, I was both excited and scared. I was thrilled to be meeting the little guy I had been talking to through my tummy. Never having had even minor surgery, I woke up that morning panicked. I made my way out of my bedroom, greeted by the sight of my mother at the top of the stairs, moaning and holding her head and her stomach at the same time. Before she caught sight of me, I ducked back into my room. By the time I'd steeled myself to join the others, Mom was already complaining to Joe's parents about her stomachache.

Without missing a beat, Muriel said, "Don't worry, Louise. They have doctors there. Let's go."

So, on this particular day, instead of calling 911, I thought better of it, and called Joe from the bedroom. As soon as I got the words "chest pains" out of my mouth, he said, "I'll meet you at the hospital," and he was gone.

I decided to drive myself to the hospital, so I tiptoed past Mom's room into the garage before she had a clue as to my absence. Even if she saw my car leave the driveway from the window in her bedroom, she'd be too late to catch me.

Still struggling for breath, I spotted a police car in a parking lot a couple of miles down the road. I stopped and asked for an escort. Instead, I was ordered to sit down, stay put. Before I could object, I was shuffled into an ambulance for the rest of the ride.

An hour later, I was still sitting in a wheelchair, waiting for an EKG. I figured no one must have thought I'd had a heart attack, or I would have been attended to.

Joe had obviously been delayed by something more important at the office than his wife dying of heart failure. I never knew when—or if—he got to the hospital, because after getting the results of my EKG, I was released. I had to call a cab to get back to my car.

To his credit, Dr. Peters, my general practitioner, had Eastern medicine sensibilities. I scheduled a follow-up appointment with him, and as I climbed off the treadmill in his office, just slightly out of breath, he said, "You're fine, Nancy. You had a panic attack. You have to learn how to breathe. Here's the name of a meditation instructor. Go, or you *will* have a heart attack."

Why do doctors like to say "heart attack" so much? What I was experiencing was not so much an attack; it was more of an onset. A giving out. An affliction. Any of those terms would have been more accurate. I think they teach doctors how to scare people on their first day of med school.

I stuffed the number in my purse along with all the other stuff I'd forget to do. Grocery lists never filled, a download of exercise routines never started, lipsticks in colors long out of vogue, gum dried up and stuck to the bottom of this bottomless satchel.

CHAPTER 30
WELCOME TO THE HOTEL CALIFORNIA

What does hell look like? I can tell you because I've been there. It's an unsolvable puzzle, a never-ending cycle, a dark hopeless pit. You can't leave but you can't stay. You can't give up, because the ones you love the most still need you.

When you wake up, you curse a little, you slap a smile on your face, drag yourself through the most necessary parts of your day. And you drink yourself into a stupor and you cry yourself to sleep. And the next day it starts all over again.

That's how the next several years passed for us. I know it was nine years, from the day we brought George home to the day he went to live in the group home, because once the dust had settled, I did the math.

"Merry Fucking Christmas." I had taken to answering the phone exactly the way I felt.

Not that too many people called anymore; just salespeople. Once they heard my greeting, they never called twice. I'd alienated everyone who ever meant anything to me, except for Joey. For him I kept up a facade—or so I thought.

Christmas was the worst holiday ever. George couldn't take the excitement; couldn't regulate his need to go to Mom-Mom's, the nickname all of the grandchildren used for Muriel. Joe's family didn't expect us until one p.m., but by six a.m. George had torn through the wrapping on all of his gifts and everyone else's, oblivious to the contents, and was demanding more.

Joey would open presents, swallow some breakfast, and sequester himself in his room. I didn't blame him. I would have done the same thing if only George wouldn't have followed me.

My husband, however, was a creature of habit. He loved ritual and tradition. I would have skipped all of it but for the fact that it allowed Joe to believe things were normal, if only for a night.

Since we were first married, Joe had decided that Christmas Eve was his night. It was his chance to show off his culinary skills to his parents, even though he could only make a few dishes. Beef Wellington was one of them. He did it magnificently, but afterward it always looked like there had been a murder in our kitchen.

Every Christmas Eve, Joe would go to the office, for a little while. I was left to gather his supplies, prepare the sides, set out appetizers, prepare dessert, and set the table. Somehow, he could never manage to be back to the house before four p.m. By then, I would be frantic.

Once we had adopted George, I would be crazed from talking him down all day or calming his rages. I either took Joey to church without Joe, or we skipped it entirely, something my older son was only too happy to do. Somehow, by the time Joe's parents came in at 6:30 p.m., things looked holiday-ish. It was very important to Joe to show his parents that we were stable, even though he knew we weren't.

The Spanish have an expression: *El qué dirán*. What will they think?

It was the mantra of the Thomas family. In their town, everyone knew of them, knew who they were. Joe's paternal grandparents had "come over on the boat" from Lebanon, and had prospered in Perth Amboy. Rumor had it that their first night on American soil, this young couple was so poor that they slept on a park bench. Starting with nothing, the family worked hard, produced many children, and bought up a large portion of real estate, landing a home on each of their nine children as they successively married.

The family businesses were varied, but consisted mainly of real estate offices. If you bought or sold a house in the greater Perth Amboy area, you knew the Thomas family, and they knew you.

This generation, Joe's parents and his aunts and uncles, were hell-bent on fitting in, being the picture of the perfect American family. That meant no fussing, no fighting, no acting up in public. The Thomases were a rock in the community, deeply rooted in service organizations and known for their kindness and generosity. Appearances meant everything to them.

I didn't have the energy to keep up this facade.

Joe's parents made it clear to Joe that I should be helping in the office; it didn't look good for his law school-educated wife to stay at home. It wasn't fine with them.

The Thomases also made it clear that when they had company and our family was there, George was to be given anything he wanted, just so there would be peace. Never mind that five Coca-Colas would mean I'd be on the floor calming George just a few hours later. It wasn't the fact that he was drinking so much soda; it was the idea that George knew that all the soda was kept on a special shelf in the garage, and he was to be given freedom to help himself. Never mind that he was patting everyone down for their cell phones. George was in charge and he couldn't handle the lack of structure.

Pretend you don't see it, and pretend everything is fine.

I couldn't pretend, so I stopped going there. Which was fine—with me.

Now, we were engaged in a dance, a whirling circle of Joe, his parents, and me. Every time I was in the company of Joe's family, Muriel wanted to know what I was doing to upset George so much that he had to hit me.

"I gave you the reports. Did you read them?" I would ask.

"I don't need to read them. There's nothing wrong with George. You just don't know how to talk to him." Muriel was convinced.

Then the phone calls would start.

Muriel would call her husband, Joseph the elder, in his real estate office. "Our son could use some help. He's overwhelmed in his office. What is Nancy doing all day? She has a law degree and she's not using it. Why isn't she in the office helping our son?"

From his real estate office, Joseph would call my husband at his office. "I just got a call from Mommy. She wants to know why Nancy isn't in the office helping you."

Joe would call me. "I could really use your help in the office. What are you doing all day, anyway? The kids are in school most of the day."

During one such exchange, as I searched for words to even begin to respond to his ridiculous request, the doorbell rang.

"Hold on," I said to Joe, and set down the phone.

It was our neighbor, the old farmer who had lived next door since before there were bedroom communities and all the damn yuppies had moved in. He was standing in my doorway in his overalls, my brindled mutt Bella being led by the collar with his left hand.

The door was wide open.

Wait a minute. When had I last come in the house? It had been hours since I'd come back from the store. I remembered that as soon as we'd come in, Joey had taken off for his room, mumbling something about running away from home. Or sending George back to Romania. Or how annoying it was to have a brother he didn't want, didn't ask for, didn't need. *What were you thinking, Mom?*

George had been demanding something I wasn't willing to give him. Candy? The TV remote? What the hell was it? I was reaching back through my day, getting nothing. I knew I'd gotten the groceries put away because for a change, there was no ice cream melting on the kitchen counter. But I didn't remember the motion of opening or closing cabinet doors.

"Is this your dog?" the farmer asked. "I found her wandering down the street. I didn't want her to get hit by a car."

Clearly this farmer had crops to plant. Or harvest. He was getting impatient, babysitting my dog while I tried to re-create my day.

I mumbled a thank-you and how I wouldn't let it happen again, and took Bella from him.

I went over to the phone and hung up on Joe to give my panting dog some water and to secure the front door.

If the Thomases wanted to know why I wasn't in the office helping Joe, they were about to find out.

Then I sat down at the computer and started an e-mail:

Dear Thomas family,

Leave my husband alone.

This has got to stop, and it is going to stop now.

Since we brought George home, we have not had one minute of peace, or help from any one of you. You want to know why I'm not in the office? The answer is simple. It's because most days, I can't remember my own name, let alone how or why to practice law. In case you haven't noticed, we have a problem on our hands—a big one.

My husband is struggling to keep a roof over our heads, and he doesn't understand why I won't go into the office and help him. You won't let him see that while he's in the office, I'm fighting for our lives.

You think George acts out because we don't know how to talk to him, that I am somehow incensing him. I've offered you the medical reports, all of them, but you decline to read them. Yet you continue to insist that George isn't really disabled, that he will outgrow it. All of it.

You think we don't love George enough.

If we didn't love George, I wouldn't have spent years scouring the East Coast, looking for solutions, for George and for the rest of us. Now, we know we have none. It doesn't make us love George any less, but it doesn't make life easier, either.

I don't remember any one of you showing up to occupy George, so that Joey and I could get a few minutes for second-grade homework. Or third- or fourth-grade. Where were you when I was sitting at the table for hours with Joey, trying to get his homework done with George practically in his lap?

The only help I've gotten with George has been from strangers, other mothers I meet in the grocery store, and the State of New Jersey. And I had to fight for that.

I was so desperate for some relief that I took George to your cousins, RoseMarie and Alice, both of whom spent their entire careers in special education. They offered to spend time with George, to have him swim in their pool, to review our records. When you found out I had gone, instead of embracing me for reaching out to family, you berated me, and forbade me to ever go again.

When I got respite, a safe place for George to stay while I took Joey on an outing, you were enraged. "How dare you do that to my grandson?" was spit at me. But you didn't offer to help.

Where were you when I was sending Joey to camp, to lessons he didn't need, to friends' homes I didn't like for him, just to get him out of George's line of fire? Or when my son was trying to protect me from being pummeled by his little brother? When Joey's childhood was withering away in front of me, where were you?

We need some time, and I expect, at the very least, for you to respect that.

It is obvious that you are not going to help us. Because if you helped us, you would have to admit we have a problem. Since you are not going to help us, leave us alone.

Leave my husband alone.

We are very busy just trying to survive.

Nancy

I sat on that e-mail for three days. Except for the time Muriel and I had that screaming match over the respite home incident, I had never spoken to Joe's family this way. I had never spoken to anyone that way. I slept on it, mulled it over, let Susan read it. When she said, "Nancy, all I hear is the pain in your voice," I hit send.

When Joe came home from work that night, I was feeling victorious. Although I knew it was improbable, I allowed myself to entertain the idea that Joe would be bringing me roses. Or at least *Thank you for sticking up for our family.* After all, Joe's family had been badgering him, too. Instead, he was furious. I had never seen Joe this angry, so I had no idea what was coming. He paced. He yelled. He even cried.

"My father was so upset he couldn't speak" were the first words he managed to get out.

That hurt. My father-in-law was a kind man. It wasn't his fault. His wife led the charge, not him. He's just a man who wants a peaceful marriage, so he does what his wife wants him to do.

"It's all true. What did you want me to do?" I said. "Keep pretending that everything is okay? It's not. It's not now, and it never will be."

I let it all out, but Joe wouldn't accept my explanation.

It took several months. Joe cajoled, begged, and threatened me until I issued apology after apology, one to each of his sisters and their husbands, and finally, to his beloved parents. They were wrong, but Joe didn't care. I had hurt his mother and father, and he wouldn't stop hounding me until he felt I had made it right. Or as right as it could be after that.

I found myself talking to God. *You sure are taking your time bailing me out of this one.* He was taking so much time that I figured He had forgotten about me. Or stopped caring.

I decided to pass the time waiting for God to show up with the only hobby that made the wait bearable. Wine. Wine became my friend, my mentor, and my salvation.

CHAPTER 31
MY WHIRLING DERVISH AND HIS MANTRA

A couple of weeks later, feeling even more humiliated and defeated by Joe's family, the panic set in again. Struggling to catch my breath, I dumped my purse and sifted through the detritus of my life. It was time to take my doctor's advice and learn how the hell to breathe. A crumpled scrap of paper emerged, and I dialed the number. It wasn't long before I found myself giggling through my first lesson in meditation.

When I burst through the door of a modest second-floor apartment, ready to calm the hell down, a small man in a cassock greeted me. He was visibly startled by my entrance. I've disturbed his karma.

He led me through a kitchen that was barely wide enough for both of us to walk side by side, so I followed him. No need to upset the atmosphere any more than I already had.

His wife Donna was already leading a small group of students through a breathing exercise, instructing them in taking breaths all the way down to their diaphragms. There were five of us now, and that meant we were almost toe to toe lying on the floor of the skinny room that served as this couple's living room and dining room.

"That's right. Breathe from down in your belly button. Remember—no breath, no life."

After a few weeks, I started to look forward to these sessions, the nervous giggling replaced by excitement for the few moments of tranquility that I could rationalize for myself. After each session, Hafizullah would greet us in the kitchen, having spent his time laying out the food that each student was expected to bring, along with his own Middle Eastern delicacy, stuffed grape leaves or baba ghanouj, a tasty roasted eggplant dip. It was a lovely courtesy, and I took it as an excuse to linger in the calm just a little longer.

Once I'd learned how to enter a room without scaring the bloody hell out of this gentle soul, he started to open up. Hafizullah is a Sufi priest. He taught me that his way of praying was to dance in praise of God. The faster the turn, the deeper the meditation. The cassock, the red hat with the tassel—he was an authentic whirling dervish. He was the calm within his own storm.

Over the course of those sessions, I came to see Hafizullah as a friend. We would chat on the phone, always for a few brief moments. I was aware of my brutishness, my charged energy, and sought to preserve his peace. We were Facebook friends and, when I really needed his advice, I would post a question, a general hypothetical, or I would ask him for insight into the meaning of life. That was his clue that I was in trouble. I assumed this gave him a cushion, a moment to collect himself, an opportunity to steel himself against my desperation. But the phone would always ring a few minutes later. He would give me a nugget of advice or a quote from his favorite poet, Rumi, loaning me a small piece of his calm world.

It was a Monday morning in early May, almost nine years after George became our family, although it felt like fifty. It was a crisp northeastern spring day. The world was coming back to life, in spite of me and my winter attitude, and pinks and reds were everywhere. The world seemed full of possibility, if you still believed in that sort of thing. I didn't. So, when the sun shone like it had nothing better to do, I felt like it was mocking me. I had been sitting at the computer after two hours of struggling to get George out of the house. It was one of those days when the bus driver was threatening to leave with a two-minute warning.

Not today.

I wasn't going to be stuck with George at home all day, starting out in a full rage. Or driving him for forty-five minutes over interstate highways to his school. I was still recovering from having George home all weekend.

Mondays were earmarked just for recovery. It was Tuesday before I could even think of arguing with George's caseworker, or teacher, or the State of New Jersey. I had to summon every bit of energy to wrestle George onto the bus, depositing his shoes with the bus aide. His vest in place, latched to the seat belt, escaping from this was the one puzzle George couldn't solve.

Joey attended St. John's High School because his dad went there. The student body was 100 percent male. They wore uniforms, with ties. It was private, prestigious, and expensive. We were painting a portrait of the perfect family, but George wouldn't cooperate.

Joey didn't like riding the school bus. He said it was beneath him. That the ride was too long. He couldn't do his homework on the bus, because the ride was too bumpy. And he was sick of seeing the same neighborhoods, in the same way, every morning. Most days, he just missed the bus. Whoops.

Really, I think he was embarrassed by his brother. He didn't want to take the chance of George being anywhere around when the bus picked him up for school or dropped him off at the top of the driveway. So, most mornings, Joe would drive him the forty-five minutes to St. John's, in the opposite direction of his office, and then backtrack to work.

Joey preferred that his father take him to school because I knew the bus route. If I drove Joey, I would inevitably catch the bus driver at the corner of Somerset Street and Easton Avenue. The red light always seemed to work in my favor. I would honk to catch the driver's attention. Sneering at me with a look of mixed humiliation and hatred, Joey would slam my car door and climb aboard the bus.

Joey wasn't happy; neither was I. With all the other indulgences I gave my older son, I still needed time to recover from George. Every morning, I had to teach my body how to breathe. That takes time.

I had been researching alternative living arrangements for George. We were frayed from not having any help. George seemed to be getting stronger by the day, and I was tired of getting beat up. He was almost fourteen years old. I was afraid that he would become more formidable once puberty set in, and there were signs that George was about to go from disabled child to disabled man.

The waiting list for group homes was ten years long. The emergency waiting list, seven. In order to qualify for the emergency list, you had to be able to prove that either your spouse was disabled or deceased, you were both of advanced age, or one of you was deathly ill. Even someone as determined as I was couldn't pull any of that off, and in seven years we could all be... well, dead.

I had found a psychiatrist for George that I liked. Dr. Patel didn't just write us prescriptions and send us home. Although she always wore a lab coat, Dr. Patel dressed in pastels, and sensible shoes. Her black, poker-straight hair and her lilting accent gave away her Indian heritage. It was almost like singing when she spoke, and I found it comforting.

She tried to engage George; she asked him questions, observed his behavior—in other words, it was a real appointment. We discussed the benefits and potential side effects of certain medications. She wanted to know his reactions, and adjusted his prescriptions based on my feedback and her observations of George. And as George grew, Dr. Patel and I started to discuss long-term options. We knew our family couldn't continue this way. I was becoming resigned to the loss of normal family life as I knew it. Although I was seeing a positive effect of the medications on George and we were all sleeping through the night, I still didn't have any help. Even medicated, the rages were becoming harder to control; George was getting stronger, and Joey was stepping between George and me. I was worried that my older son, so big and strong, could hurt George while trying to protect me. Or worse, I was worried that Joey would consider himself responsible for my safety, the third adult.

When George got too big for me to put in a protective hold, the school behaviorist told me to turn the doorknob on his bedroom door backwards, so that it could be locked from the outside, so that I could keep George contained during his rages.

During one of our sessions, when Dr. Patel broached the subject of a group home, I was ready for the discussion. Although I had dismissed the idea early on, and continued to fight the idea, I was physically and emotionally exhausted. She explained things as many times as I needed to hear them. She told me that group homes were not the old mental health institutions of my nightmarish imagination; they were homes in neighborhoods, where specially trained staff checked on the residents on a regular basis. The workers went home after an eight-hour shift and came back the next time, refreshed, rested, and, most importantly, patient. The residents became like family to each other. They were well cared for, socialized, trained in appropriate behaviors and activities of daily living, like making their beds, doing laundry, and preparing simple meals.

When Dr. Patel convinced me that I wasn't doing George any favors trying to keep him at home, I was ready to figure out the how. By now, I knew I couldn't wait ten years, or even seven.

"What about the waiting list?" I asked.

"If George is an immediate threat to himself or others, there is a way. The next time George attacks you, call the police. It will be documented."

Calling 911 was not an option. Joe wouldn't allow it, saying "I will not have DYFS in my business." Even though we had all the methods we were advised to implement well documented, he didn't want to take a chance on having the police call the Division of Youth and Family Services, the state agency charged with the protection of children and vulnerable adults. Also, Joe was well known in our community. He often represented clients in municipal court, so all the police officers in town knew him. A pillar in our community, Joe was an active member of the local Rotary, a past Exalted Ruler of the Elks Club, a fourth-degree Knight of Columbus. Joe simply would not allow the negative attention.

I went back to Dr. Patel for other options. "If he is admitted through the psychiatric ward of the hospital, the waiting list has no meaning," she said. "That doesn't necessarily mean involving the police. Don't worry. The medical staff are professionals. They'll know what to do."

So, there I was, staring at the computer that Monday morning, when Hafizullah popped onto Facebook. I hadn't said anything, but the phone rang. It was my Sufi priest.

"Are you okay?"

"How did you know?" I asked, although I knew the answer. "I have a weird feeling," I said.

He said, "I know. I want you to write down this mantra and repeat it all day. Don't worry, Nancy. You will be okay."

Something told me to pack a small bag. I put George's socks, underwear, pajamas, and a change of clothes in an overnight bag, a robot, taking directions. As though if I had thought about it, I would have fallen down and not been able to get up. I was following orders from my subconscious, mechanical and rote.

Just as I placed the bag in the trunk of my car and walked back into the house, the phone rang again. It was the principal of George's school.

"Mrs. Thomas, the bus is going to be late bringing George home. It took us an hour to get him onto the bus. He's had a rough day. You should be prepared."

Before I could object—"How could you send him home in that condition?"—the school principal was off the phone.

Standing in my driveway was Joe Smalley, the township director of transportation.

"What are you doing here?" I asked.

"I got the same phone call you did" was the reply. "I came to see for myself."

The doors opened.

George was standing on the top step of the bus, all sweetness and light.

From the dazed look on the bus driver's face, the switch had just flipped back to calm. Mary, George's kindly gray-haired bus driver, looked frazzled. Her hair was disheveled, her eyes were wide, and she had tears in her eyes.

She handed me George's shoes. "I confiscated them after he threw them at my head."

Highway 78 was a long and treacherous enough road to negotiate without having to dodge shoes being thrown from the back of the bus.

"Hi, Mom."

CHAPTER 32

IT TAKES A VILLAGE . . .
OR THE ENTIRE HOSPITAL STAFF

"Get in the car, George."

"Where?"

"We're going for a ride."

We walk into the emergency room of Somerset Hospital, George holding my hand. I ask for the psychiatric ward, and the intake nurse acts like I'd just asked her for the time, saying, "Have a seat right over there. Someone will be with you shortly."

George asks for a Coke from the vending machine, and I hand him a bag of chips to go with it. As he sits down to enjoy his usually forbidden sugar and caffeine-laden snack, I'm beset with panic.

I haven't prepared any explanation. What should I say when this calm child walks into the psych ward? Would they take me instead? Perhaps they should.

I finger the crumpled piece of paper with the mantra in my pocket, pray a little, and wonder if I'd simply imagined this entire day—the past nine years. Maybe *I'm* the crazy one.

I call Joe at the office and tell him to come.

It doesn't take long for George to morph into his own personal storm.

We are admitted to the psych ward for evaluation.

During his calm moments, George manages to get the nurses and security guards to fall in love with him. He figures out that the badges the security guards wear on a type of lanyard also operate all the doors.

A six-foot-two guard is standing over my child, smiling. George leans in for a hug, and Tyrone complies. With lightning speed, George reaches out, pulls on the badge, and flashes it at the double doors.

He's off and running through the emergency room, poking his head into all the bays, touching the elderly, the infirm, shaking hands with strangers, before he's caught and corralled.

So far, only George's teachers and Joe and I were handling George. We knew him and loved him. Watching strangers handle my little boy in this environment was horrifying.

I can't understand why Joe is too busy to show up at the hospital. I imagine him having lunch in some air-conditioned restaurant or chatting on the phone with his mother. I had called him hours ago, and he had yet to arrive.

As a child in the psychiatric ward of the hospital, George is not allowed to be alone. One of us is required to be with him at all times. The only thing for us to do is watch the TV hanging from the ceiling.

Joe and I are taking shifts. Since I'm with George all day, I demand that Joe come and spend the night with him. When I arrive the next morning, Joe looks fully rested. Even with all the screaming and ranting outside, the fact that he and George are being confined in a room with bars on the window, and the lock on the outside, Joe says, "Yeah, I slept great. Just going home for a shower. I'll be at the office."

It's our second day in the psych ward. George is having his third full-blown rage since we arrived. He has been shot in the thigh with Thorazine, a drug used to sedate elephants. Two hours in, he is still trying to climb into bed with the other patients.

By the weekend, there are so many drunks and drug addicts coming into the psych ward that they're lined up in the halls. For George's safety, we've been locked in a holding cell, where we have to get an attendant's attention to get in or out.

I've given George the remote and I sit there, imagining myself anywhere else. Joe arrives sometime after dinner for his second night's restful sleep with his son. As I drive home, I'm wondering if I'm the crazy one.

It is the morning of our third day at the hospital when I meet Cathy, an angel disguised as a social worker. Her white hair is pulled back in an efficient-looking bun. Her lack of makeup and tie-dyed T-shirt over acid-washed jeans make me think she's never left Woodstock.

Cathy speaks to George and me in soft tones and listens to all I have to tell her, as though I'm giving her my grocery list. We meet with her in the holding area, and she disappears quickly afterward.

An hour later, George is welcomed into the pediatrics department of the very same hospital, with all the pomp and circumstance of a visiting dignitary. They place an alarm on his ankle in case he tries to escape. He already has the doors figured out; all he needs is an unsuspecting victim.

When Cathy comes upstairs to check on us, I say, "How did this happen?"

Her only answer is "We couldn't leave George there," but I know she's gone to bat for us, to provide George with as much comfort as a hospital can deliver.

I am now free to leave George for short periods since he is safe and in no danger of escaping. Visitors are allowed, as well as George's teachers and therapists, and he begins receiving compensatory instruction and physical therapy.

A few days after George has settled in, I go home to meet with the Division of Developmental Disabilities to begin discussing a more permanent solution for George.

When I return, I find George holding court. Several of his cousins are in his room, obviously just arrived.

As I round the corner, George's head pops out and he calls his nurse.

"Pat," he says, "ice cream. Juice. Everybody," his arm making a big circle around his room, so she shouldn't misunderstand.

I watch in awe as George runs his fiefdom. Treats appear on demand. Visitors and service providers appear at his bedside. Who would run away from this?

Nurse Pat hands me my purse, saying "Go home, get some rest—we've got this" as she walks me down the hallway. Tears well up in my eyes when she guides me onto the elevator and pushes the L button.

As the doors close, muffled yet unmistakable, she says "And I don't want to see you until tomorrow." Another angel.

CHAPTER 33

EVEN THE MAYOR
CAN WEAR OUT HIS WELCOME

When he's not raging, George is actually quite engaging. Behaviors that are normally considered inappropriate in social settings are taken as charming. During our stay at Somerset Hospital, George has probably hugged everyone in range at least a dozen times, and patted each of them down for their cell phones, and introduced himself. The whole staff seems to have fallen in love with George, especially the big security guard he conned out of his door pass. So, every time there is a Code Gray in Pediatrics, the code for psychiatric emergency, the entire hospital staff knows that George is having an episode. My instinct is to rush to his side, to place him in a protective hold, the way I'd been taught. Instead, I am not so gently shuttled out of the room and told to wait outside, curtains closed against me.

Unnerved, there is nothing for me to do but imagine George, frightened, raging, and being handled by strangers. Treated with drugs, not human contact.

Mothers are supposed to fix everything, right?

I can't fix this. I am an epic failure as a mother.

During one of these episodes I am sitting on a bench at the end of the hall, folded into myself, sobbing at my incompetence.

The elevator doors open and Tyrone, the security guard from the emergency room, appears.

"Hi, Tyrone. What are you doing here?"

"I heard the code. I just wanted to make sure my little buddy was okay."

"Okay," I manage to squeak out. "I'll wait here," pretending I have a choice.

With that, Tyrone is off, leaving me a wet, sobbing, helpless mess, until he returns to reassure me. The kindness of this man, a victim of George's escapades, who comes running to check on him every time he goes into a rage, leaves me in a heap.

As ironic as it may seem, I have learned that every one of George's disabilities has a silver lining. The greatest blessing of George's combination of disabilities is that once the rage is over, it's over for George. He has no memory or hangover emotion.

In the twenty minutes I am required to wait down the hall, I've aged a hundred years.

When I'm finally allowed to see him, George is bellowing for a snack.

"Hi, Mom. Ice cream?"

Even a child as beloved as George wears out his welcome sometime.

The first week, our social worker works diligently to find a place for George. The procedure in these situations, I am told, is to get the child into a short-term rehab facility, talk them through the emergency, satisfy themselves that the child is no longer a threat to himself or others, and send him home.

Every phone conversation with one of these facilities ends with "I'm sorry, Mrs. Thomas, we can't help you. If your child's IQ were a little higher, we could take him. We could talk him through it."

There is no talk therapy for a child with limited intelligence and no impulse control. They are telling me something I already know.

Now that the hospital realizes that there is nowhere safe to send George, they are starting to talk about financial responsibility. Up until this point the hospital and the social worker have been working out George's stay to fit within his insurance coverage. But now we are running out of time. There is no treatment being rendered by the hospital that justifies him remaining here, and once each potential treatment facility realizes that George can't be fixed with a short stay, they turn him down.

The welcome mat is disintegrating under our feet. If we don't leave the hospital soon, we will be presented with a bill. A big one.

I get Dr. Patel on the phone.

"Don't leave the hospital without a solution," she says. "Stand your ground. The State will figure it out."

I am determined but out of ammunition.

I have Joe in the office of a special needs attorney in Princeton before he can get a grip on his wallet. She tells us that the board of education should place George and then we wouldn't have to fight for permanent housing once he reaches the age of twenty-one. Letters start to fly between our new attorney and the board of education.

Armed with this new information and some help, my determination gathers steam. We have come so far and we're so close to getting somewhere. If I turn back now, all will be lost.

My mother-in-law's nine years of accusations echo in the recesses of my memory.

What are you doing to my grandson?
You just don't know how to talk to him.
Are you sure he's handicapped?

"Shut up!" I shout.

Joe's "What did you say?" makes me realize I've said it out loud.

I am swirling with conflict. We can't bring him home, but we can't leave him at the hospital.

Dr. Patel's advice plays on the next track: "You're not doing George any favors by keeping him at home. He needs more help than you can give him."

George has been in the hospital for two weeks. We have no solution, but now I find myself sitting at my dining room table with Frick and Frack, the caseworkers from the State of New Jersey who had been assigned to assist me in finding help for George. I had called Joe hours ago, but he still hadn't come home.

So, I go into battle alone. Again.

They are trying to convince me that there is nowhere for George to go—that he needs to come home. I'm trying to convince them that, without staff, he cannot come home. He is a danger to himself and to us, his family. I have proof now, and I have questions, but I also have an idea. George had been spending odd weekends at a respite home in the next town. It had taken me years to find out about this opportunity and to get him approved by the State. Once I'd found the New Jersey statute and quoted it to George's caseworker, she had relented and begrudgingly given us the thirty days a year of respite to which we were entitled. He was close enough to home in case there was an issue, or we needed to get to him quickly.

"Why can't George stay at the respite home until we find a permanent placement for him?" I knew these two caseworkers didn't have much power, but getting some extra time approved could work. I had learned about this in conversations with other special needs moms—our "secret handbook," as it were.

"We don't have the authority to approve that, Mrs. Thomas," they say, almost in unison.

"Well, who does?"

"We don't have that information, Mrs. Thomas." Another pat answer.

I am running out of patience with these two, and I finally explode.

"Why won't you help me? It's like I'm in the middle of the street screaming for help and you are ignoring me."

"We can't answer that question, Mrs. Thomas. Do you have any other questions?"

How can these two say this stuff with a straight face?

"Yes. Who is going to be responsible when George hurts himself or one of us?"

"We can't answer that question, Mrs. Thomas. Do you have any other questions?"

Yes. How quickly can you get the hell out of my house?

As they drive away in their government-issued sedan, I wonder who, indeed, will be responsible if George hurts one of us.

It's a bright day in early June. I'm alone, on my way to the hospital to collect George, admit defeat, and take him home. The sun is always shining on my failures, and today is no different. We have run out of options. There is no solution in sight, no hope, when my cell phone rings.

It's Frick from the State. Or Frack. I can't remember which; I get them confused.

"Mrs. Thomas, we've come up with a temporary solution. We received approval to let George live in the respite home until we can find a permanent placement for him."

I fight the urge to scream *That was my idea, you idiots!* and replace it with "Thank you."

I'm given instructions. An ambulance is on the way to transport him. Just like that.

A tidal wave of relief washes over me. It's a Band-Aid on a gaping wound, but a Band-Aid nonetheless.

In the parking lot of the hospital, getting out of the car, my knees give out. I pretend to be looking for something I've dropped while I struggle to catch my breath. No witnesses, thank goodness. Except for the crying jags at the end of the hall during bouts of Hurricane George, I've been holding it together pretty well in front of the hospital staff. I'm still Mom; I'm still under the illusion that I'm fixing things. I'm still in charge, dammit.

What I do know is that I'm in charge of nothing, but I can't let on or the floor will crumble beneath me, and I will be swallowed into an abyss.

George is heralded out of the hospital with all the attention he has come to expect. Word is out among the staff, and as he is wheeled out of Pediatrics, the halls are lined with well-wishers. George, chubby from three weeks of all the ice cream and cookies he could demand, is grinning and high-fiving security guards, nurses, and aides.

George thinks it's a treat to ride in the ambulance. I'm not allowed to go with him, so I follow in my car to the respite home.

Two weeks later, and I am still waiting for a permanent solution for George.

School is out. Mom is on a rare outing, to Connecticut, to visit my sister.

And I am reveling in the company of my cranky older son. Even his moodiest moments are a treat for me. Giving Joey a safe place to fall is my only goal, and I try to temper his anger with all the indulgence I can muster.

He and I are standing in the aquarium in Ocean City when my cell phone rings. It's my mother, and she's calling from a pay phone in the Trumbull Mall. She had been resisting the idea of a cell phone of her own, so I make her call me from her destination whenever she travels by herself more than a couple of hours away. My mother is still insisting on driving herself around, and the image of her tiny white-capped head peeping over the steering wheel, getting pulled over on the Merritt Parkway for driving 85 miles an hour in a 55-mile-per-hour zone makes me giggle.

She is also resisting hearing aids. She asks where we are, and I answer, "Joey and I are at the beach."

"What?" she squawks.

Before I can make my way outside, I yell into my phone, "We're at the seashore." The entire room turns to look at me.

"You had to take a detour?" came her response.

On the rare occasions when we are all at the dinner table together, my husband has taken to moving his mouth without making any sound when speaking to my mother. This joke never fails to amuse him, even though it annoys my mother.

Joe has a dry sense of humor. He's quiet by nature, and not prone to telling jokes. But when he does loosen up a little, he's quite funny. Once my mom realized that Joe was making fun of her, she couldn't help but smile. She knew she needed to have her hearing loss attended to, but still refused.

My son Joey and I have our own little shorthand jokes, and this one makes it into our repertoire immediately. Whenever I would say "seashore," Joey would immediately respond with "You had to take a detour?"

It breaks us up every time.

By the time my mother could say "What are you two laughing at?" we'd be on to something else. Not sharing our little secret ribbing of her makes it that much funnier.

CHAPTER 34

SUMMERTIME AND THE LIVING . . .

As the summer wears on, there is still no permanent solution for George.

Without a permanent solution, the State of New Jersey has been forced to suspend the thirty days of respite rule. I have been using the respite home as my own little babysitting service. Just ten minutes from home, I pick up George for treats or ice cream whenever I miss him, being careful not to keep him too long, lest it appear that I can handle him at home.

I'm worried that the respite home will get tired of catering to George. They have no real behavior plan for him in place, and he is left to wander around the house at will and watch as much TV as he wants. There is no one here trained in protective holds, because this place is intended as a short term break for parents, a couple of days at a time, a weekend. So, George is left to his own devices. I thought it odd that one day when I went to visit him, George answered the door. It took a full five minutes for the caregiver to even realize I was in the house.

But this was the first time this had ever happened. Several phone calls to Mirlaine later, and I am satisfied that this was a mistake. I am assured that the caregiver has been dealt with, and I assume she has been fired or reassigned. So I have no choice but to chalk it up as an aberration.

With George out of the house, my mother now thinks I live to drive her to the mall. She wants to go back and forth so often, I dub her "Returns Are Us."

Growing up, my mother took it upon herself to be my style mentor. I resisted her advice because she would never let me buy what the other girls were wearing. The skirts I wanted were too short or cheaply made. Despite myself, I absorbed it. She knew how to stretch our clothing budget; she had to, as she liked to shop. A lot. Louise taught me about weft, and how to tell if a garment was well made and would last. She also told me to never wear horizontal stripes. "They make hippy girls like you look wider, Nancy."

No wonder I couldn't enjoy my body. Sophia Loren was sexy, but there were more girls on the covers of magazines who looked like Twiggy. Vanity always came before comfort.

When I was a little girl, my mother would take me along whenever she needed a dress for a special occasion. She loved to shop at Lillian's, a dress boutique where you got waited on like royalty. I would sit on the tapestry settee in the showroom and the salesclerks would cluck over me and tell my mother that one day they would dress me, too. And wouldn't I look beautiful. I fantasized about the day when I would finally be old enough to twirl around in their chiffon and feather gowns.

When she found something she liked, my mother would call me into the dressing room, either to zip her up past the girdle she always wore, or to lament over her thighs. "If I could only take a knife and slice this off," she'd say.

It stuck. Once, long after I grew up and Lillian's went out of business, I caught myself in a dressing room mirror, echoing the very same words.

Osteoporosis made mother hunched, and she used a walker for support. When faced with the reality that she couldn't make it on her own from Macy's at one end of the mall to Lord & Taylor at the other, she relents and lets me rent a wheelchair from the kiosk.

Today, my mother has decided that she needs a new pocketbook. We find ourselves in the purse department at Macy's. Louise directs while I run bags to her for her approval. If this one is too big, the next one is too small. The next one is too heavy, and the one after that is flimsy. She finally settles on one as I begin to run out of options.

Joey likes to come with us for his own entertainment. He's pushing the wheelchair. Pretending to run toward the descending escalator with my mother sitting in it provides endless fun for him, but my mother is not amused. Nor is she happy when Joey piles our purchases on her lap so that we don't have to carry them. She mutters *Mannaggia diavolo*— Damn the Devil. But she puts up with it. She's out of the house and has our attention.

Finally home, my mother goes to her room with her new purchase. When she emerges thirty minutes later, the purse must be returned. "It's really more money than I wanted to spend."

Running back and forth to the mall with my mother every day is not my idea of fun.

I take the opportunity to put the two Joes in the car for a drive to Florida. It's been a couple of months since George went to the respite home, and, except for the one time that he answered the door, I have finally satisfied myself that he is safe. But we still don't have a permanent place for him.

About an hour into the trip, Joe's cell phone rings. As he hangs up, he pulls the car over to the side of the road.

"George ran away," he tells me as he turns the car around.

The fear that swirls as we head in the other direction mixes with the guilt of yet another failure as George's mother.

Two miles later, Joe's phone rings again. George has been found. A police officer is driving him back to the home.

The officer thought he would give George a treat and let him ride in the front seat and press the siren button. As it turns out, George can even best a cop. With his lightning speed and innocent face, George reached over and changed gears while the car was in motion. George arrives back at the respite home locked in the back of the police cruiser, where they transport the suspects.

Joe pulls the car into a diner to discuss what to do next. Do we go home or continue our trip? What good are we going to do at home? He can't come home with us, but we don't want to leave him. From a booth in the corner, I spend hours on the phone with the respite home supervisor, until we are satisfied that safety precautions are now in place. Locks with keys have been placed on the doors from the inside. The keys are safeguarded. It is impossible for a child to leave the home unsupervised.

We continue our trip, but I am almost constantly on the phone, pressing for a permanent placement to be found for George.

The response I get is a litany of phone calls from the lowest-hanging fruit. The State of New Jersey has decided that I am an inconvenience and they try to place George in the first group home that has availability and is willing to take him. I know this because the first phone call I receive from one of these homes goes something like this.

"Hello, Mrs. Thomas. This is Ms. Atkins at Brookhaven. We would like to invite George over for dinner to meet his new roommates."

This is the first time I have heard the voice of Ms. Atkins. This is the first time I have heard of Brookhaven. George does not have roommates until we agree he has roommates. At Brookhaven. With Ms. Atkins.

By now, I have Mirlaine, our caseworker at the Division of Developmental Disabilities (DDD), on speed dial. Except she has now been replaced by BethAnne. When BethAnne tells me that Mirlaine has retired and that she would be taking her place, I imagine that I drove Mirlaine running from the building. I entertain myself with the thought of Mirlaine curled up in a corner, rocking back and forth, replaying our phone conversations in her memory, and mumbling "Have a blessed day. Have a blessed day. Have a blessed day."

Ever since Mirlaine and I had come to our little agreement that I wouldn't call her supervisor if she answered my phone calls, my caseworkers seem to take my calls the first time. Maybe BethAnne has been clued in, as well. Now that we that we had our own legal advisor, DDD was making motions that looked like they were cooperating. But that didn't mean they had to be happy about it or make it easy for us.

I knew that the State couldn't move George without our approval, and that we, George's parents, had final say over the choice of an appropriate group home for our son. I let BethAnne know that I knew this, and that we were not just going to deliver George to Brookhaven without vetting the agency that was going to care for our son.

There are several more phone calls that summer, all similar in tone. I assume that we are being offered the least expensive options first.

I do not relent. I'm not trying to get rid of George; I am looking for competent people who can help him. DDD is not going to give in easily, but neither am I.

CHAPTER 35
HELP? THANKS. WOW!

School is back in session, and now George is being met by the bus driver at the respite home. I am no longer required to fight George onto the bus, nor am I required to take his beatings. The return of the pressure of having to follow directions, to get dressed and on the bus on time, is frustrating for George, and he is back to the frequent rages that plague him. Except I am no longer the object of his aggression.

I'm still visiting whenever I want, to have a few peaceful moments with my little boy, to assuage my guilt, and because I can.

George's respite workers aren't trained for a permanent resident; they are trained to give families of special needs children a break. It doesn't matter if they don't enforce a structure or a set bedtime. The children are made to feel as though they, too, are on vacation.

Now with the added pressure of keeping George on a schedule so that he gets enough sleep, is fed, washed, and dressed for the bus ride, and kept under control in between, the respite home unwittingly becomes my advocate. They are complaining that their resources are stretched. It's also expensive, and the State is tired of paying for it. George's stay is eating up all the money earmarked for respite.

But I'm winning our game of chicken; I know that if I bring George home, I will lose everything I've been fighting for, on George's behalf as well as ours.

Finally, we are starting to get calls from homes that want to meet George for purposes of assessing their fit for each other, not just move him in blindly. The professionals who run these homes have looked at his records and checked to make certain their staff was professionally trained to handle George's needs. Now they are ready to evaluate whether they would be the right fit.

Brookhaven doesn't make the list, but several others do. We look at several throughout the state. So far, The Elms is at the top of our list. It is an hour and a half from home, further than the forty-five minute drive we were expecting. But, the staff has assured us that they would be willing to deliver George halfway when we wanted to bring him home. The group home looks like a house, not an institution, just like any other house in the neighborhood.

When Joe and I take George for a preliminary visit, an aide greets George and takes him on a tour of the facility, leaving us free to interview the group home supervisor. We are shown the bedroom where George will sleep if we decide to place him there.

The home is sparsely furnished, but well kept. There are always two caseworkers on hand. The children's safety is paramount, so anything they could hurt themselves with is not allowed in the house. The walls are decorated with posters of cartoon characters the residents enjoy watching on TV. There is a chart on the refrigerator with picture prompts for the day's schedule: a toothbrush, then a shirt and pants, breakfast, a school bus. There is another menu chart with pictures of food. The Elms is conversant in protective holds, behavior modification, and the benefits of limited sensory input on children's outbursts. They have ample staff and a structured, predictable day-to-day routine. A structure we, his family, can't provide for him.

The staff falls in love with George. The first thing he does is sit at the kitchen table. "Snack," he demands, and is offered a Jell-O cup. He picks a red one, his favorite.

Tears well in my eyes as the light dawns. All this time, these people were here, knowing what to do for our child, what he needs to calm down, to thrive, to feel—and be—safe.

Joe and I weigh the options. Even with the distance, this place feels right. We decide The Elms will be his new home.

CHAPTER 36
GUMMY BEARS AND PINK FROSTED DOUGHNUTS

It's early November, almost exactly nine years since we brought George home. I'm at the computer, typing an e-mail.

Dear friends and family,

It is a cloudy, wet, blustery afternoon. We've just driven in a rainstorm to George's new home. The weather matches our moods.

Today, our son George took up residence at The Elms Group Home, buoyed on the ride by gummy bears and pink frosted doughnuts. When we arrived, he inspected his new room, found it to his satisfaction, and sat himself down at the kitchen table, demanding the red Jello.

Confident that he would be well cared for, we left George in the capable hands of his caregivers. He waved good-bye to Mommy, Daddy, and Joey, and embraced ToriLynn and Tom, hugging them with all his might, showing no sadness at our leaving.

Our failures on George's behalf are many, our attempts to mainstream him well-meaning but futile. So now, with heavy hearts and faith in the decisions that have brought us to this place, we give George the greatest gift we can give him. We as a family are unable to monitor George twenty-four hours a day, without a chance to recharge. We are unable to give him the structure he needs for an appropriate daily life.

George now has staff to care for him, each one arriving refreshed and intact to work for just an eight-hour shift at a time. And for that, we are grateful.

We as a family were abused by his aggression, though he could not control it or understand it. George will now be trained by professionals who will defuse his violence and teach him new behaviors to replace the old.

We will no longer have food thrown at us. George will be taught to use utensils appropriately and sit at the table. We are hopeful that one day we can all enjoy a meal together as a family.

George continues to be our beloved son, our treasured family member, and we now have hope that someday, he will be able to function in a peaceful, loving manner. Our wish is that you will understand and continue to support us as we support and guide George on this next phase of his development.

There are pink sprinkles on the backseat of the car; there are gummy bears stuck to the upholstery. I think we will leave them there for now.

Nancy, Joe, and Joey

CHAPTER 37
THE END . . . OR THE BEGINNING

From the permanent impression on the sofa booms the voice of my sixteen-year-old son Joey. "Mom, do we have any batteries? The remote's dead."

"I'll check," I say, pretending exasperation, but secretly happy for any interaction with him.

Seriously, Joey? You've been home for a month now and you still can't muster the energy to move your carcass off the sofa to walk across the room? Is summer break over yet? No wonder the batteries are dead . . . Watching TV is all you do.

That's what any decent mother would have said. Any decent mother would have let him find the batteries for himself or do without, but I was no decent mother. I had long ago thrown out that handbook.

I leave the pot I'm tending on the stove and make my way to the dreaded junk drawer. Out comes the usual debris of a busy family—receipts for items long ago discarded, dried-up pens without any sign of matching caps, several decks of playing cards, each with one or two missing, an old lipstick in Coral Cream. Thank goodness that shade went out of style a long time ago.

Batteries always hide in the back, and as my fingers reach into the furthest recesses of the chasm, they clutch a familiar shape. I feel it before I see it: a silver cross, the chain broken.

It's too late. The reel begins to play before I can push it away. Clutching the cross, I sink to the floor and fold into myself, hot tears streaming down my face as the scene plays in my mind.

The school bus pulls into the driveway. The sound of the tires crunching along the fifty feet of gravel seems to last for an eternity. I'm torn over whether to open the wine now. Maybe today I wouldn't need it. Maybe today would be okay.

I'm holding my breath when the bus door opens. An angelic little boy alights, smile on his face. As he waves good-bye to his bus driver, I think *Maybe today won't be so bad.*

We enter the house as I chatter away nervously. "How was your day, George?"

As the door shuts behind us, his twisted expression is my answer. Hazel eyes turn to ebony, rage seeping out of every pore of his little body.

I say "No, George . . . no, George—don't hit."

Arms flailing, he attempts to punch me, but I manage to duck the flying fist. And then another. As his fingers scrape my neck, he gains purchase on the cross I'm wearing, and it flies off into a corner of the room. I am left with a souvenir, the tracks of his fingernails on my chest.

The echo of Dr. Federici's voice: "I know they didn't tell you this, but children with fetal alcohol syndrome, like George, are notoriously violent. He needs to be in a facility that can handle these challenges."

The arguments last late into the night.

"You can't do that to my child," Joe says.

I argue back. "It's the only way. Can't you see what this is doing to us? George is going to hurt one of us, maybe badly next time."

Finally, mercifully, the reel exhausts itself.

My shirt is soaked with tears. A final sob, a deep breath, and I right myself.

I dry my face and pick up the phone.

A young woman answers, "The Elms Group Home. This is Shondra. May I help you?"

"Hello, Shondra. This is Mrs. Thomas. May I speak with my son?"

We are about to have the same conversation we've had several times a week for the year since George went to live at The Elms.

"Hi, George, how are you?"

"Good." The answer I have come to expect from him every time I ask.

"How was school today?"

"Good." Same answer every time.

"What are you doing, George?"

"Cookies. Oven. Hot. Me."

"Oh, you helped Beth make cookies? Ooh, nice. Be careful."

"Saturday. Me."

"Yes, honey, I'll see you Saturday."

George has run out of interest and conversation for me. "Bye, Mom," he says, and hangs up while I'm still saying, "I love you, George."

The phone lands in the cradle with a comforting kind of thump. The endless hours of negotiation with state agencies and care providers, the months of research and all the sleepless nights—they all fade into the background as I remind myself of the progress this little man has made, how he is safe, secure, well cared for, and loved, and how he will always own a corner of my heart.

As this feeling of gratitude washes over me, my head rests against the wall, my body remembering how to breathe. I feel gratitude for the help that will enable George to grow and thrive, gratitude for the return of some semblance of home life, which enables Joey to be the typical lethargic American teenager he happens to be this summer.

I plop onto the sofa next to my big lazy adolescent and land a big one on his cheek before he can push me away.

"I love you, Joey," I manage to squeak out.

"Ewww, Mom. Gross. Did you get the batteries?"

EPILOGUE

George taught me many things, but the most important is this. It's a funny thing, believing in a higher power. For almost a decade we struggled to overcome and deal with his challenges, the violence and disabilities with no discernible rhyme or reason, the search for answers, the finding of none. It all seemed meaningless. God, creator of the universe—whatever label you put on it, when life is good and you're on top of the world, it's easy to say, "God's got my back."

When things get really dark, that's when your faith gets put to the test. I am ashamed to say that, in my darkest moments, I felt like mine failed me. Every day, I wondered, *Where is the blessing in this mess?* What had I done that I should be punished while I'm still walking the Earth? And what about all the innocents who got hurt while I was busy trying to save George? My son Joey, the little boy who'd had a disabled, violent child foisted on him and was expected to act like everything was just A-okay?

I had carried a feeling of peace ever since the day my father died. Words that had never come naturally to me—"I love you, Daddy"—turned out to be my very last words to him. I took that moment as a sign that everything was going to be okay from that point on. It was a blessing, that God had allowed me to say the most important thing in the world to the most important person in my life, at the last possible moment I would ever have the opportunity to say it.

Right up to the moment when George first hit me, I thought I was invincible. Maybe I always went off half-cocked because I knew, with as much certainty as I knew the sky was blue, that God wouldn't let anything really terrible happen to me. I was fearless to the point of being reckless. I lived my life without a safety net because I figured I didn't need one.

I almost killed myself with alcohol, trying to dull the pain of incompetence, failure, and guilt. I almost killed myself trying to insulate my older son from the horrors that had become our home life.

I did a pretty good job. I made sure Joey had lots of outlets. I let him slack on chores. I let him do things and go places I never would have, had I been in my right mind. Maybe I indulged him too much, but I was making up for a lot.

He knew what was going on, including with my marriage. In fact, when I divorced my husband, the only person who was surprised was Joe.

When I was about to leave his father, I walked into Joey's room and perched on the edge of his bed. He had completed his first year of college and was home for summer break. I sent up a trial balloon.

"Joey, what would you say if I told you that Daddy and I weren't going to live together for a while?"

I was expecting to have to cushion the blow with ice cream, or beer. Instead, unruffled, he said, "What took you so long, Mom? You guys have been divorced for years."

For a long time after George went to live in the group home, I spent a lot of my time staring up into the sky. My prayer was always the same: *Dear God, you asked so much of me. I did it. I did what you asked me to do. I have no more to give, so please, just let me die peacefully.*

I would tell my friends not to stand too close to me. They thought I was joking. I was not. I figured now that I'd outlived my usefulness on Earth, there would be a lightning bolt coming out of the sky at any moment to claim me. I didn't want any more collateral damage.

Life isn't easier now, it's just different. I still live by the seat of my pants.

I divorced Joe and moved to Florida, by myself, once my mother was gone and the dog died. George was safely ensconced in the group home, and Joey was in college, permanently out of the house. There was no one left for me to take care of every day, no one who needed me. I left a twenty-four-year marriage and made my way toward an uncertain future with no plan, no real money. Just the knowledge that somehow, everything would be okay.

Joey has grown into a man. A man with scars, but a man I am incredibly proud of. He is kind, centered, responsible, empathetic. He emerged from his childhood an old soul, victorious. The world is a better place because of who he has become.

George is thriving. He is the best George he could ever be. He's in a structured environment. He has his own staff. He still rages, once in a while, but I only hear about the episodes now. The time I have with him is sacred, and fun. The blessing of reactive attachment disorder is that he doesn't pine for me when we're apart. He doesn't miss anybody. Whoever meets his needs at the moment is his favorite.

Joe was in a serious relationship within a few weeks of our separation, and married her, the first woman he dated after me, within a couple of years of our divorce. I still say "I love you" when I talk to the father of my children on the phone. I believe and hope that he is happy.

I took another bar exam and am now licensed to practice law in two states. I have my own home, where nobody throws tomato sauce on my chandelier or peanut butter on my ceiling.

Everything is okay.

I guess faith won out after all.

ACKNOWLEDGMENTS

Two words hardly seem adequate to express such an enormous amount of gratitude, but, somehow, they say it all. Thank you to those who convinced me that my story needed telling... to Steve Eisner and the team at *When Words Count*.

Thank you to the mentors who helped me along this path... Dr. Ronald Federici, Susan Anderson and Hafizullah Sufi. Thank you to all the mothers who gave me information and encouragement in shopping malls and grocery stores.

Thank you, Kari Hunter, for reading, rereading, and reading some more during weekends when you would have liked to be doing something else.

I will always be grateful to my focus groups, new friends in Myrtle Beach, old friends at the Gemini, and Lake Park Business at Breakfast. You were courageous enough to point out flaws at the risk of hurting my feelings. You made the writing better.

Thank you, Woodhall Press, for believing in the importance of shedding light.

And thanks to Pete.

To my ex-husband and my two fabulous boys... not only did you travel this road with me, but you allowed me to tell about it, in my own words.

Thank you, Paul Welsh... because the greatest gift you can give someone is allowing them to acknowledge your help.

Finally, and most importantly, thanks, God, for not leaving me... ever.

ABOUT THE AUTHOR

Nancy Ferraro is a winner of the national writing competition, *When Words Count*, and the author of *When the Bough Breaks*. She rediscovered her love for the law as an estate and trust attorney in the Palm Beach area.

She is known for sharing her life experience with her clients and friends, to shed light and share hope. Ms. Ferraro has been published in books and periodicals throughout the country and is currently at work on her second memoir.